A PIECE
OF THE WIND

And Other Stories to Tell

Ruthilde Kronberg

and

Patricia C. McKissack

1817

HARPER & ROW, PUBLISHERS, San Francisco
New York, Grand Rapids, Philadelphia, St. Louis
London, Singapore, Sydney, Tokyo, Toronto

FIRST EDITION

Library of Congress Cataloging-in-Publication Data
Kronberg, Ruthilde
A piece of the wind, and other stories to tell / by
Ruthilde Kronberg and Patricia C. McKissack—1st ed.
p.   cm.
Summary: A collection of stories intended to be told, drawn from a
variety of traditions including European, African, and contemporary
American. Includes tips on such aspects of storytelling as voice
patterns, body expression, and audience participation.
ISBN 0-06-065364-7
ISBN 0-06-064773-6 (pbk.)
1. Tales. [1. Folklore. 2. Storytelling.] I. McKissack, Patricia
II. Title.
PZ8.1.M465Pi 1990
398.2—dc20   89-29738
                                                              CIP
                                                              AC

90 91 92 93 94 FAIR 10 9 8 7 6 5 4 3 2

Contents

Part Three

Stories to Act Out, 69

Part Four

Stories for All Occasions, 111

Introduction

Telling stories is one of the oldest teaching devices and one of the surest ways of keeping a group entertained. Since the dawn of history human beings have been gathering under shade trees, on front porches, and around hearth fires to listen to storytellers weave incredible yarns about brave and foolish people, events grand and simple, and places as near as next door or as far away as forever. And the tradition lives on.

We tell stories for the same reason our ancient counterparts told them: to teach, to entertain, and for the pure joy of it. It is through stories that children first learn to unravel life's complicated patterns and to understand their own and others' culture, history, customs, values, and beliefs.

Most of the stories in our collection are not well known. Some were created just for this book; others have been collected over several decades. Whether found in a dusty old book or told to us by a friend, each story was chosen for its age-old wisdom or for its humor and playfulness. Whenever we found a story that touched out hearts, we included it here.

The question we are asked most frequently as storytellers is, how do you develop a story? There is no pat answer; there is no right or wrong way to approach it. We can only offer suggestions. Use what you can and discard the rest.

Because verbally transmitted stories don't have the benefit of illustrations, as do stories in books, the storyteller must rely upon sensory details, unusual voice patterns, whole body expression, and audience participation. A storyteller's own talent and experiences, combined with life and joy, help give a story a special quality that no other storyteller can give it. That is what makes a verbal story different from a book. Tales from the oral tradition often change from one storyteller to the next.

You don't have to tell the stories precisely as we have *written* them. Consider these stories as models — patterns from which you can design a new story that is uniquely your own. For example, one story begins, "Once upon a time, a wise shepherd boy lived among the sheep on the hillsides." The opening scene can be enhanced greatly by adding a few well-placed words. Noting that this is a German folktale, you might begin, "Once upon a time, a wise shepherd boy named Hans lived among the sheep on the grassy slopes just outside a small Alpine village."

Sometimes we do not give characters names but use instead "the mother," "the old man," "the brother," "the wife." That doesn't mean that you shouldn't give them names. We leave that up to you. Remember, what we have provided is the story pattern.

There is no absolute in telling except the absolute that you should *never memorize*. Familiarize yourself with the words and the chronology of events and maybe even memorize transitional phrases, but never, ever memorize verbatim.

Note that most stories have four basic elements: character, action, setting, and idea. Help the listener visualize the story characters by assigning them distinctive personality traits, mannerisms, and tags — anything that clearly defines who the characters are. For young children delineation between good and evil characters is essential. Show young audiences how a kindly old man walked, how the wicked king sat on his throne, or how a carefree young girl skipped along.

But character development is not enough. When and where the story takes place is an important element too. Take time to learn about the story's background. And set the stage for your young listeners by telling them what it was like to live in a faraway place or a time gone by. When setting is well developed, the listener can be magically transported through time and space.

Action gets the audience's attention and holds it. A story without movement is generally not successful. Keep your characters doing something. But keep in mind that no matter how strong a character is, where the story takes place, or how much action is involved, if the idea—the message—is not handled properly, the story won't work.

Avoid overstating the "moral of the story." The children's responses generally will let you know if the message has been conveyed. Let the listeners come to conclusions without being told what to think. Allow them to exercise their analytical and critical thinking skills.

Children don't like predictable or didactic answers. They have an insatiable appetite for knowledge, but they don't want information spoonfed to them. They enjoy being "shown" solutions. They appreciate being given options. And above all, they like problem solving.

A good storyteller acts as a guide. An excellent story is one that allows the child to think and reenact the content over and over and, in so doing, to grow and learn.

Once you have chosen a tale suitable for the occasion, where do you go from there? If you are a beginning teller, we suggest you tell the story at least once before presenting it to an actual audience. If you have no audience, tape the story and listen to yourself speak. (Don't worry, we never sound to ourselves as we sound to others.)

What you want to listen for are two things. First, does the story have rhythm? Does it flow evenly and smoothly? Second, does the story have good concrete details? Can the audience see, feel, hear, and smell what is going on? If not, perhaps you need to add some colorful words at just the right place to get the effect you want.

How do you know if the tale is working? If it catches the imagination of the children, you will be able to hear a pin drop. If it doesn't, the level of restlessness rises.

Remember, you don't need experience, but experience is the best teacher. To become an effective storyteller, you must practice telling. The more often you present the story, the more confident you become with it. The story will change and grow and even take on a personality of its own. If you love it and give it with joy, your audience will respond in equal measure.

Part One

STORIES FOR EASY TELLING

These easy-to-tell stories come from all over the world, and they show us how we are alike in spite of our cultural differences.

We have tried to write the stories the way we tell them, and you are free to tell them your own way. You need not memorize them word for word to tell them well. To learn a story you've chosen, read it through several times. It may be helpful to jot down on a card the names of the characters and a brief synopsis of the plot— beginning, middle, and end. Try to picture the story as it is happening. Imagine what you might see, hear, smell, feel, and taste.

Then practice telling the story in your own words. Expand the story by adding details or dialogue. Above all, share your own delight in the story with your audience.

A Piece of the Wind

In a village in Africa lived Tor, the proud father of a boy named Mooka. Whenever Tor looked at Mooka, he vowed to be a faithful father and to teach his son all the wisdom he himself had learned from his parents.

When Mooka was old enough to be taught, Tor called him to his side and said, "Mooka, I want you to grow up wise and good."

Mooka laughed and replied, "Father, I am already wise and good."

"Mooka!" said the father. "The only one who can say that of himself is God's Son."

"Leave God's Son out of this!" responded Mooka arrogantly. "All I want you to know is that young people get wiser faster these days, and we no longer want to be bothered by the wisdom of our parents."

Tor understood that his son could not learn unless he wanted to learn.

Not long afterwards Mooka fell in love with Yamini, the daughter of a wise village elder. Mooka went to the elder and said, "I would like to marry your daughter Yamini. What is the bride price?"

Yamini's father replied, "I don't care much about money, but I do want my daughter to be married to a wise and good man. The bride price for my daughter is a piece of the wind."

Mooka knew right away that he was being tested and

that he did not know the answer. He went home to his father and told him what had happened.

Tor laughed. "You have always boasted how wise you are. If you really want Yamini to be your wife, put a knife in your belt, take a gun and a hunting bag, and find a piece of the wind."

Mooka did as his father told him, but hard as he tried, he could not catch a piece of the wind. He sat down on a tree stump and thought a long time. Perhaps he should look for another wife? No, he decided. He really loved Yamini.

After a while he went back home to his father. "I have been foolish not to realize how much I need your help," said Mooka. "Will you help me?"

Tor smiled. "Of course I will help you."

Together they went to Yamini's father, who greeted them and offered them food.

But Mooka's father asked for only a glass of water. After he was given the glass, he studied it for a long time. At last he said, "Forgive me, my friend, but why have you given me water that has not been ground and sifted?"

"Where do you grind and sift water?" asked Yamini's father.

"At the same place where you get a piece of the wind," replied Mooka's father.

Yamini's father smiled and said to Tor, "When I told your son to bring me a piece of the wind, I knew he could not do it. But now I see that he is a wise young man. He had the wisdom to ask his father for help. Everyone knows that a man who honors his father and mother will honor his wife. I welcome Mooka as my son-in-law."

Mooka and Yamini were married. And when their children were born, they taught them to honor the wisdom of their parents.

The Woodpecker

A beggar woman named Katri was forced to wander through the villages and towns of Rumania begging for alms. Her fate made her very angry, and as she walked along the roads, she often argued with God. "It's your fault that I am in such misery," she would say. "Why don't you give me a chance to change my luck? Am I not as good as anyone else?" But God never seemed to listen to her.

One day Katri saw an old man sitting by the side of the road. A sack tied shut was lying next to him. The beggar woman was hungry, and when she saw the sack, she thought the stranger might have some food inside. She stopped and said, "Good man, can you spare a bite to eat?"

"I have some bread in my pocket," replied the man, "I would be happy to share it with you."

"May God bless you for it," said Katri, and she sat down by the stranger's side. The old man took a piece of bread out of his pocket and gave half to Katri.

While they were eating, Katri asked, "Are you waiting for someone?"

"I am waiting for someone to throw this sack into the ocean," the old man said matter-of-factly.

"Why do you want that sack thrown into the ocean?"

"There is a good reason for it," the old man assured Katri.

"Have you already chosen someone to throw the sack into the ocean?" asked Katri.

"No," replied the old man. "Anyone who promises not to open the sack will do."

"The ocean is close by," said Katri. "If you offer a good reward, you won't have any trouble finding someone to do it."

"The reward will be great for the person who does what I ask," the old man explained. "She will never have another worry in life. But the punishment for opening the sack is terrible."

"I would like it fine if I never had another worry in my life," said Katri. "I will take the sack to the ocean."

She reached for the sack, but the old man stopped her and said, "Not so fast! I must make sure you understand that it will be very bad for you if you open the sack."

"I have ears in my head!" said Katri crossly. "Why should I care what's in the sack? You can trust me. I always keep my promises, and I promise not to open it."

"So be it," said the old man, and he handed Katri the sack. The beggar woman threw the sack over her shoulder and walked toward the ocean.

On the way she had to pass through a forest. Just before she entered, she looked back and saw that the old man was no longer in sight.

"That old man is a fool!" Katri exclaimed, laughing. "How will he ever know I opened the sack if he doesn't bother to keep an eye on me? I certainly would never tell him if I opened it."

She walked a few steps farther and sat down in the shadow of a tree. As she rested, she wondered about the contents of the sack. She touched it with her finger. It felt as if it were filled with dry grass. Why would anyone want to throw a sack filled with dry grass into the ocean? Katri wondered. Before she knew it, curiosity overcame her, and she untied the sack.

But alas, it was not filled with dry grass. There were thousands of insects inside, and the minute they saw the daylight, they hopped, flew, crawled, and jumped out of the sack and swarmed off into the forest.

"Shoo, shoo! Get back into the sack," cried the old beggar woman. She chased after the insects, but it was too late. As she dashed around trying to catch the bees and the caterpillars, the mosquitoes and the grasshoppers, her nose turned into a bird's beak. Her arms turned into wings. Her dress and her hair turned into feathers. Her legs became the spindly legs of a bird. Indeed, the reward for opening the sack was as terrible as the old man had said. The old beggar woman Katri became a woodpecker.

The children of Rumania know her story, and whenever they hear a woodpecker's voice in the forest, they sing:

Kwirr, chaw, Katri woodpecker.
Why did you open the sack?
Go knock your head against the tree
Make sure it doesn't crack.

Your Room, My Room

Jean and Joan were twins, and they had always shared a bedroom with their two older sisters. But now that the Petersons had bought another house, Jean and Joan had their own room.

The house was old, but the rooms were large. Jean and Joan's room had two big windows that overlooked the backyard, and it had a large closet. Their room needed to be painted before their furniture could be moved in.

"You may decorate your room any way you like," their parents told them.

The girls enjoyed sharing their plans.

"Now that we have our own room," said Joan, "I'm going to decorate it just the way I want."

"Now that we have our own room," said Jean, "I'm going to decorate it just the way I want."

Although the girls were twins and looked alike, they liked different things. Jean liked reading, but Joan liked writing. Jean liked soccer, but Joan liked bicycling.

Joan stood by the window. "I'm going to put my bed on this wall," she said.

Jean stretched her arms wide. "This is where I'm going to put my desk and shelf," she said.

They both looked in the closet. "Which side do you want?" Joan asked.

"Since you're left-handed and I'm right-handed, why don't you take the left side, and I'll take the right," Jean replied.

Everything was going smoothly until they had to decide on a color for the walls.

"I like yellow," said Joan.

"Yuk," shouted Jean. "Yellow walls! I like blue better."

Joan shook her head. "No way. Blue is boring."

"Yellow!"

"Blue!"

Jean and Joan argued about blue and yellow all morning.

"Come with me to the paint store," Mother said. "Maybe we can find a color both of you like."

The paint salesman showed them hundreds of color samples. Jean and Joan had never seen so many colors.

"Blue, yellow, and red are the three main colors," said the salesman. "By mixing two or more colors together, we can make any color you can imagine."

"I still like yellow," said Joan.

"I still like blue," said Jean.

The salesman went to the storeroom. He returned with two small cans of paint, one yellow and one blue, two brushes, and a piece of paper. He gave both girls a brush and paint can. He told Joan to make a yellow circle. He told Jean to make a blue circle on top of the yellow one. They were surprised to see the yellow and blue mix together to become green.

"Oh, I like green," said Joan.

"I like green too," said Jean.

They decided to paint their room green. It was a color that made Joan happy, because it was part yellow. It was a color that made Joan happy, because it was part blue.

The walls were painted, and the furniture delivered.

"How about polka-dotted bedspreads?" asked Jean.

"I like checks," Joan answered.

"Dots."

"Checks!"

"How about stripes?"

The Wise Shepherd Boy

Once upon a time a wise shepherd boy lived among the sheep on the hillsides. He was poor in possessions but rich in wisdom. People came to him from near and far to seek answers to their questions.

One day the king heard of the young shepherd and sent for him.

"I will treat you like my own child," said the king, "and you shall live with me in my palace if you can give me an answer to three questions. Tell me, how can I count all the drops in the ocean?"

The shepherd boy thought for a while. Then he answered, "Dear King, have all the rivers on this earth dammed up so not one single drop runs into the sea. Then I can count all the drops and give you an exact answer."

The king nodded his approval. "That was a good answer. Now tell me, what is the sweetest thing on earth?"

"Sleep," answered the shepherd boy. "People can go without food for a long time. But if they are not allowed to sleep, they will soon lose their senses."

"Indeed you are right," replied the king. "Now answer my third question: How many seconds of time are there in eternity?"

"I can answer that question only by telling you a story," replied the shepherd boy. "Somewhere—no one knows where—stands a Diamond Mountain, which is two miles high, two miles deep, and two miles wide. Once a year a tiny bird comes and sharpens its beak on it. When that mountain is worn away, the first second of eternity will have passed."

After the king had heard the third answer, he asked the shepherd boy to come and live with him.

The shepherd boy shook his head. "Permit me to go back to my sheep," he said. "Only there in the hills can I think clearly."

The king understood the shepherd boy's request and allowed him to go back to his sheep. But whenever the king needed advice, he went to visit the shepherd in the hills.

Tante Tina

The city of Husum in the northern part of Germany is the home of seafaring folks. Every year when the water between the shores of the North Sea and the Island Nordstrand freezes solid, the people of Husum get together and celebrate their winter festival. Merchants come from near and far. They set up tents and sell marvelous toys and delicious foods. Bands play old, beloved tunes, and both the young and the old come to skate, to dance, and to eat and drink to their hearts' content.

One year a lame old widow, known to all as Tante Tina, did not feel well enough to come to the festival. But she could lie in her bed and watch the merrymakers from her bedroom window, because her small frame house stood on a high wall by the sea.

Toward evening Tante Tina noticed a small dark cloud in the west. It frightened her. Her dead husband had been a ship's captain, and from him she had learned that clouds like that were the sign of an oncoming storm.

Terrified, she opened her bedroom window and cried, "A storm is coming! A storm is coming! Get off the ice."

But the music was so loud that no one heard her feeble voice, and the bright lights from the festival kept the people from seeing the dark cloud.

As the cloud grew bigger and bigger, Tante Tina knew

that soon the wind would change from the north to the west, and within a short time the storm waters would come and break up the ice. Unless someone could attract the attention of the people on the ice and bring them to shore, every man, woman, and child would be swallowed by the icy waters of the North Sea.

Tante Tina's poor old heart beat like a drum. Already she could feel the dangerous warm breeze. Full of fear, she began to pray as she had never prayed before.

Suddenly her heart grew calm and she knew what to do. She crept out of her bed and went over to the stove, where she grabbed a piece of burning wood and hurled it into her bed. Almost immediately the straw mattress exploded into flames.

By the time Tante Tina managed to crawl out of her house, she heard the people cry, "Fire! Fire!" as they rushed off the ice to put out the fire. Just as the last people came safely to land, the storm broke loose. The warm winds caused the ice to crack, and thick black clouds obscured the light of the moon. Only the burning house of the brave old woman shone like a beacon in the darkness and helped the terrified people find their way safely home.

Soon the flood came and washed away the tents, tables, benches, toys, and whatever else was left behind. But not one life was lost, thanks to Tante Tina, who had sacrificed everything she owned to save the lives of her friends and neighbors.

The King's Cathedral

There once lived a mighty king who decided to build a cathedral. When the wealthy merchants and nobles of his country heard about the king's plan, they came and offered to contribute money.

The king refused their offering. "The cathedral will be built using my money," he said. "No one but I must contribute."

When the cathedral was finished, the king asked his mason to put up a sign that read:

> May it be known to all that this cathedral
> was built for the glory of the Lord Almighty
> by King Philip III.
> anno Domini 1214

People came from near and far to see the cathedral, and everybody praised the king for his faith and generosity.

But one morning the king's steward ran into the king's bedchambers. "O Sire," he said, "a prankster has erased Your Majesty's name from the sign in front of the cathedral and replaced it with another name."

"Whose name?" the king cried angrily.

"With the name of the poorest woman in town," replied the steward. Now the sign read:

May it be known to all that this cathedral
was built for the glory of the Lord Almighty
by the spinning woman Marie.

The king was annoyed and commanded the steward to
set things right, which he did, and once again the sign told
about the king's noble deed.

But not for long. The following morning, people read
for the second time that Marie the spinning woman had
built the cathedral.

Now the king was furious. "Who is doing this?" he
cried. "I want three guards to watch the sign day and night."

For the third time the king's name was engraved on the
sign.

When his name disappeared again, in spite of the
guards, the king realized that the name had not been
changed by any human hand. He sent his servants to look
for Marie.

When they brought Marie before the king, she trembled
with fear.

The king spoke kindly to her. "My good woman, do not
be afraid. Only tell me the truth. Did you hear my order
that no one but I was to give money for the building of the
cathedral?"

Old Marie fell on her knees. "Have mercy on me, O
King," she sobbed. "I am a widow, and I earn my living by
spinning and knitting for the wealthy. I have very little
money, but one day I had an extra penny, so I went and
bought a small bundle of hay and threw it on the street so
the oxen who pulled the stones to the building site could eat
it. I did not mean to break your law, and I know nothing
about the changing of the name. Please forgive me."

Marie's words touched the king's heart. "You have done

nothing to forgive," he said. "It is I who have to learn from this. I know now that it is God who is teaching me this lesson. I will change the wording of the sign and ask God to forgive my pride."

The king kept his word and the new sign read:

> Beware of practicing your piety before men in order to be seen by them; for then you will have no reward from your Father who is in heaven.
>
> —Matthew 6:1

Now That I Have a Green Thumb

Juan sucked his thumb, even while he was sleeping. Some people told him, "Big boys don't suck their thumbs." Other people said, "You'll be going to school in September. You can't suck your thumb then."

But Juan didn't feel very big. Besides, it was January, and September was a long way off. So Juan continued to suck his thumb.

One day Juan went shopping with his parents.

"You might have a green thumb," said Mother.

"What?" Juan asked.

"A green thumb means you can grow plants well," Father explained.

Juan looked at his thumb. It wasn't green. It was the same brown color he was all over. "How do I know if my thumb is green?" he asked.

Father smiled. "We'll buy some seeds. You can plant them. If they grow, then you have a green thumb."

Juan took his thumb out of his mouth. "Maybe it will turn green if I stop sucking it," he said.

Mother laughed. She bought seeds, some pots, and potting soil. Juan planted three or four seeds in each pot. He watered them and then set the pots in a sunny window.

He waited. In eight days little green sprouts began to push through the soil.

"My plants are growing!" he shouted. But his thumb was still brown like the rest of him.

Winter passed quickly. The days grew longer and warmer. Mother told Juan when it was time for him to plant his seedlings outside.

First Juan dug the soil and smoothed it out. Then he planted the seedlings about eight feet apart. Spring rains watered the plants, and they grew stronger. Juan was careful not to suck his thumb, but it was still brown—no sign of green anywhere.

Summer came. The days grew hot. No rain fell. Juan had to water his plants. Father bought some plant food, and Juan fed his plants. He pulled weeds. Soon afterwards Juan saw a bright orange flower on one of the plants. Then another flower and another bloomed.

All summer Juan watched his garden. The plants grew into large vines. Juan also watched his thumb. But it hadn't turned green, even though he hadn't put it in his mouth for a long, long time.

When September came, Juan went to school. He met many new friends. But every afternoon he hurried home to see about his garden. Wonderful things were happening. One cool October day, Juan lifted one of the dark green leaves. He found a large orange pumpkin—and another and another. Wherever a flower had bloomed, a pumpkin had grown.

Juan took one of the pumpkins to "show and tell" at school. Everybody agreed that Juan did have a green thumb.

Kelly sucked her thumb.

"You might have a green thumb too," Juan told her.

"How will I know?" Kelly asked.

"Why don't you plant some seeds and see if they grow?"

Kelly looked at her thumb closely. "Will my thumb turn green?" she asked.

Juan showed her his thumb. "I don't know," he answered. "I'm still waiting."

Bundles of Worries, Bundles of Blessings

A woman who worried day in, day out, made herself and her family miserable with all her fears. One day she went to a wise friend. "I have more worries than anyone else in the world," she wailed. "Could you help me deal with them?"

"Only God can help you deal with your worries," said the wise friend. "Take your troubles to him and don't despair."

The woman followed her friend's advice and asked God for help. One night, she dreamed she was in a large gray cave filled with thousands of gray bundles. Some were big, some were small, and none were of the same size.

As she looked at the gray bundles, an old man came toward her and said, "These are worry bundles. All the people in the world carry one of those on their left shoulder. If you feel that your bundle is too heavy for you, put it down and choose one that suits you better."

The woman looked and saw that she was indeed carrying a gray bundle on her left shoulder. She put it down and began to search for a lighter one. She tried out hundreds of bundles until finally she found one that seemed just right.

"May I take this one?" she asked. "It feels much more comfortable than all the others."

"You may take whichever you want," the man answered kindly. "But open the bundle before you leave."

When the woman opened the bundle, she saw all of her worries inside. Well, she had picked her own worry bundle. She sighed deeply and said, "At least my own worry bundle fits me better than the other ones."

"That seems to be true for everyone," replied the man with a little smile. "But do not despair. There is a bundle on your other shoulder that should lighten your worries."

The woman looked and saw another bundle on her right shoulder. But it was not gray. It was woven from gold and silver threads, and it sparkled like a diamond in the sun. Just looking at it made her feel better.

"I wonder what is in it," she said excitedly.

"Why don't you open it?" the old man suggested.

She did and found that the bundle was filled to the top with all her blessings. As she looked at them, one after the other, her heart overflowed with thankfulness and gratitude. Full of joy, she turned toward the man to thank him for making her aware of the gold-and-silver bundle.

But the old man was gone, and so were the huge gray cave and all the worry bundles. The woman was in her own bed, and the beautiful morning sun was shining into her face.

The Mirror

Long ago in Japan lived people who had never seen a mirror. One day a man by the name of Konojo found a strange object lying by the roadside. It glistened in the sunlight and sparkled like a jewel. He picked it up and could not believe what he saw. It was a picture of his father as he had looked when he was a young man. Konojo was delighted, especially when the picture seemed to have a life of its own. When he laughed, it laughed. When he looked stern, it looked stern.

"My father must be aware of how much I miss him since he died," thought Konojo. "He found a way to send his picture to me. I will treasure it, and if I have a son of my own, I will pass it on to him."

He wrapped the picture in his scarf and started to walk home. But as he approached his house, he said to himself, "My wife Aiko was never too fond of my father. If she sees his picture, she will repeat all her grievances against him, and I don't want to be reminded of them. I will hide the picture in my father's old trunk, and when I look at it, I will remember all the good times my father and I had together."

Konojo did as he had planned, but soon Aiko noticed his frequent trips to the old trunk.

"Why are you constantly going to the old trunk?" she asked.

"I have personal things inside," answered Konojo.

"I see," said Aiko, and she wondered why her husband had suddenly become so secretive.

One day when Konojo was not at home, Aiko opened the trunk and searched for some clues to explain her husband's strange behavior. She found nothing but some books and Konojo's scarf. But when she picked up the scarf, she realized that it was wrapped around something. She unwrapped the object and saw the picture of a beautiful young woman.

"Konojo loves another woman!" cried Aiko in despair. Tears of sorrow began to flow from her eyes. She was so upset that she didn't notice that the woman in the picture was crying too.

Filled with despair, she threw the picture back into its hiding place and hurried away. When Konojo came home and tried to hug Aiko, she pushed him away.

"How dare you embrace me when you love another woman?" Aiko said.

Konojo was puzzled. "What are you saying? I do not love another woman," he said.

To prove her point Aiko ran to the trunk and returned with the picture. "Here is the proof," she cried. "For days you have been sneaking to the old trunk. It is because you were looking at this picture."

"You found the picture of my father," Konojo said. "I found it lying on the street, and I have been very happy about it. How can you say it is the picture of a woman?"

"Now I have heard everything!" said Aiko. "Do you really think I am so ignorant that I can't see the difference between a picture of your father and a picture of a woman?"

She began to cry so loudly that a priest who was passing

by heard her and came into the house. He asked gently, "Is there anything I can do to help you?"

"Yes, indeed," said Konojo. "My wife Aiko, who is usually quite reasonable, has lost her senses. She insists this picture of my father is that of a woman, and she accuses me of not loving her anymore."

The priest took the picture and looked at it. Then he laughed. "Either the two of you must have looked too deeply into a wine bottle, or some evil spirit is at work. This is clearly the picture of a priest. I will take this to the temple and keep it there. Now I beg you to stop quarreling and make peace."

"It must have been the evil spirit's work," said Konojo, and Aiko agreed. They hugged one another and quarreled no more.

The Very Good Samaritan

There once lived a man by the name of Isaac who was well known for his kindness and piety. One day he was traveling along a wild and lonely mountain trail when he heard a cry for help.

Isaac immediately searched the area and soon found a young man lying at the edge of a cliff, moaning as if he were about to die.

"Help me," the young man begged. "I was traveling along the road when three robbers attacked me. I tried to fight back, but they beat me and ran off with all my possessions."

Isaac gave the stranger some water from his jug and helped him mount his own horse so he could take the young man to the next town and care for him. But the minute the young man sat onto Isaac's horse, he rode off.

Isaac, who knew the mountain like the inside of his coat pocket, slid quickly down the steep mountainside and met the horse thief further down the road. "Stop!" Isaac commanded.

Used to his master's voice, Isaac's horse stood still.

"If you want this horse," said Isaac to the young man, "take it as a gift. I don't want you to become a thief on my account."

"It makes no difference to me if the horse is a gift or

stolen," jeered the young horse thief. "I shall sell it at the next town."

"For heaven's sake, don't do that," cried Isaac. "Everybody there knows me and my horse. When you come with that horse and try to sell it, people will think you have killed me and they will kill you in return."

"Why should you worry if I get killed?" sneered the horse thief. "It's my hide, and it shouldn't make any difference to you if I live or die."

"I don't want my friends to kill you, nor do I want you to be killed," insisted Isaac. "Listen to me. I am willing to write you a letter of sale if you promise that you will tell no one of what happened between us."

"The world is full of fools," said the young horse thief. "But so far I have met none bigger than you. Sure, go ahead and write me a bill of sale for the horse I stole from you. But I am curious. Tell me why are you acting so foolishly. There must be a trick to all this."

"There isn't," said Isaac. "But should people hear how you treated me, they might be afraid of helping a stranger who is in real need, for fear that what happened to me will happen to them. And that stranger, my friend, could be you."

The young man stared at old Isaac. Suddenly he began to cry. "My father and my father's father were thieves and ended their lives on the gallows. They taught me all they knew and never cared what would happen to me. If I could have had a father like you, I would never have become a thief."

"It's never too late," said Isaac with a smile. "Come with me. With God's help the damage of your childhood can be undone."

"I will!" cried the young man, and he moved in with Isaac and became an honest man.

The Street Sweeper

A poor peasant lost his crops to bad weather three years in a row. Because he could not feed his family any longer, he sent his wife and his daughter back to his wife's parents and went into the city to become a street sweeper. Hoping to save as much money as possible, he worked long, hard hours and spent almost nothing on himself.

When he had a small sum of money saved, he became afraid that thieves might steal it. He decided to bring it to a rich jeweler who had given him an extra job now and then. The peasant asked the jeweler to safeguard his money. In his innocence he thought that a man with so much wealth must be trustworthy.

The jeweler was more than willing to take the money. He promised to keep it in a safe place, and at the end of each month the street sweeper added more of his hard-earned pennies.

Five years passed, and the street sweeper decided he had saved up enough to go home. With a happy heart he went to the jeweler's house and asked for his money.

The jeweler looked at him in amazement and said, "My good man, what are you talking about? I've never seen you before in my life."

"How can you say that?" demanded the street sweeper. "You have known me for five years. I came to you at the end of each month and brought you my money for safekeeping."

28

"Do you have a witness?" sneered the jeweler. "If you do, bring him to my house. If you don't, you do not have a leg to stand on. Now leave my shop before I call the police."

"I did not think a witness would be necessary," pleaded the poor street sweeper. "I thought I could trust you."

"Do not bother me any longer. God only knows what you did with your money," said the jeweler. "Now leave! You are wasting my time."

"I won't leave until you give me my money," cried the poor street sweeper.

The jeweler rang a bell, and immediately two burly servants entered and threw the street sweeper out into the street. There he sat with tears streaming down his face.

Just then a carriage drove by. Inside sat a woman and her little daughter.

"Mommy," said the little girl. "Why is that man crying?"

"Hush," said the mother. "I am sure he does not want us to know why he is crying."

"But, Mommy, you always say we should help people who are sad," the child said.

To satisfy her, the mother asked the driver to stop the carriage. "Forgive me for bothering you," she said to the street sweeper. "My daughter insists that I find out what is troubling you. Perhaps I can help."

"I have lost five years of my life," said the street sweeper. Then he told her his sad tale.

"I have heard others say that the jeweler is a scoundrel," replied the woman. "Let's see if we can't get your money back. Tomorrow morning I will go and speak to him. Sweep the street in front of his house and watch for my arrival. About ten minutes after you see me enter the house, come inside and ask for your money. Do not mention what happened today, and pray that my plan works."

The street sweeper began to pray as he had never prayed before.

The woman went home and put her most precious jewels into a jewelry box. The following morning she went to the jeweler. She showed him her jewels. "My family and I just moved into this city," she explained. "But your reputation as an expert on fine jewels has already reached my ears, and I came to you for advice. My husband went on a business trip to a city far away. Yesterday a messenger arrived to say that my husband wants me to join him because his business will take longer than he thought. But he forgot to send instructions about what to do with my jewels, and I do not know what to do. If I take them along, they might be stolen. If I leave them at home, they might be stolen too."

"If I were you, I would not take them on a journey," said the jeweler. "I have a burglar-proof safe, and I would be glad to keep them for you."

"I was hoping you would say that," replied the woman. "But how will we go about it? I hardly know anyone in this town. Where would I find someone to witness our transaction?"

"There is no need for that," replied the jeweler. "You can trust me. I will return your jewels to you the minute you come back from your journey."

The woman looked at him as if she were trying to make up her mind what to do.

Just then the poor street sweeper entered and said, "Sir, I decided to go back to my family. Would you please be so kind as to give me the money you kept for me?"

For a brief moment the jeweler looked angry. But then he smiled wickedly and said, "Of course." He opened his safe, and as he gave the street sweeper his money, he said to the woman, "People come to me all the time and ask me to safeguard their money."

"I am glad there are still some honest people in this world," replied the woman. "I have made up my mind. I shall leave my jewels with you." She closed her jewelry box and was just about to hand it to the jeweler when the door opened and her maid came running inside, saying, "My lady! A second messenger arrived while you were gone and said that your husband's plans had to be changed. He will arrive within a few hours."

"What better thing could happen to me!" replied the woman. She turned to the jeweler. "Thank you, my dear friend, for offering to keep my jewels." She bowed and left while the jeweler gnashed his teeth.

The following day the clever woman invited all her friends and the street sweeper to her home. After everyone had eaten heartily, she told the story of the treacherous jeweler. Her friends passed the story on, and soon the jeweler was the most despised person in the city. In time he had to close his shop and leave because no one would associate with a man who stole money from the poorest of the poor.

The street sweeper returned to his family. With the money he had saved, he was able to restock his little farm, and they had enough to eat for the rest of their lives.

A King Seeks God

In a country far away lived a powerful king. Near the end of his life he called all his counselors to his castle.

"During my years on this earth I have seen everything a man can see, except God," he told them. "You must help me to see God. If you don't, you will be thrown into my dungeon."

No one knew how to help the king see God, so all the counselors ended up in the dungeon.

One day a stranger came to the castle. "Sire," he said, "maybe I can help you."

"Think twice before you offer your help," replied the king. "If you help me see God, I will reward you richly. If you don't, you too will end up in the dungeon."

"I seek no punishment or reward," replied the stranger. "However, you must promise to do everything I tell you to do if you want me to help you."

"If it will help me see God, I promise," the king said.

Early the next morning, just as the sun was rising, the stranger awakened the king. "Quick, quick! Look at the sun for as long as you can," he ordered.

The king stared at the sun, but within seconds he had to lower his gaze. "Do you want me to lose my eyesight?" he demanded.

"No, I do not," said the stranger. "But how do you

expect to see God if you can't look at the sun for more than a few seconds? God's face is a million times brighter than the sun, and in this life no human being can ever expect to see it."

The king liked the stranger's explanation, but he was not yet satisfied. "Tell me, what was before God?" he asked.

The stranger thought before he answered. "Again I must ask you to do as I tell you. Please start counting."

The king began to count. "One, two, three, four, five, six, seven."

But the stranger interrupted him and said: "Oh no! Anyone can do that. Start counting before the number one."

"I can't!" said the king.

"Neither can I, nor can anyone else. So no one knows what was before the beginning."

"You explain things better than all my wise men," said the king. "I have just one more question: What does God do?"

"That is the easiest question so far," replied the stranger. "Let us exchange our clothes just for a little while."

The king agreed. He took off his crown and robe, and he put on the stranger's cloak. Meanwhile the stranger put on the king's garments. Then he climbed on the king's throne and said, "God puts some on a throne and asks others to step down. Your life is coming to an end, and you will have to give up your throne soon. See to it that you are at peace with the world. Don't waste your time on things you cannot understand. Prepare yourself for the kingdom of God instead."

The king was deeply moved by the simple wisdom of the stranger. He followed the stranger's advice, and when the king's last hour came, he was ready.

Part Two

STORIES THAT
INVOLVE THE AUDIENCE

A good motto for the stories in Part Two is "Tell me, and I listen. Involve me, and I remember." All these stories provide opportunities to involve the audience in the storytelling.

As you tell the story, you may have the children repeat a refrain or chorus, or they may mime certain actions in the story.

Using visual aids, simple props, puppets, or any combination of these might help shy participants to get involved. For seating arrangements, check the instructions in the note section of this book. Teach the songs and refrains before telling the story and give the audience a cue for when they are to join in. Don't fret if it doesn't turn out perfectly the first time. Stories improve as they are shared with many different audiences.

After you've told the story once, you may ask the group to retell the story, helping one another recall the details. Many children remember the lines after hearing a story only once. If they don't, you can help them remember. Retelling the story helps children to visualize and remember, and the story becomes their own.

The Legend of Tutokanula

Once upon a time two brothers named Koda (Friend) and Kabato (Runner) went to a river to swim. But the water was so cold that they had to get out.

Back on shore Kabato began to hop from one foot to the other, chanting:

> I am so cold, I am so cold,
> I'll freeze to death before I'm old.

> *(Audience repeats these lines.)*

"You won't freeze to death before you're old," laughed Koda. "Let's race to the big boulder by the forest and lie in the sun until we are warm again."

Koda reached the boulder first. Kabato followed, but the minute they lay down they fell into a deep sleep. Meanwhile the boulder began to grow, little by little, until it reached the sky. *(The two persons who play Koda and Kabato crouch on a sturdy table.)*

Evening came, and Koda and Kabato's parents came to look for the boys. Although they searched long into the night, they found not a trace of the brothers. No one knew where they were, except the animals who had seen the boulder grow.

The next day the parents continued their search. All they found was a wounded raccoon. The father wanted to put him out of his misery, but the mother picked him up and said, "Maybe Koda and Kabato are lying somewhere wounded and helpless, hoping that someone will find them. Let me take care of the poor little creature." She took Raccoon home with her.

One day when Raccoon was feeling better, he heard the parents talking and realized that his kind friends were the parents of the boys on top of the mysterious boulder. As soon as Raccoon was well enough to return to the forest, he went to the animals and asked them to help him bring Koda and Kabato down.

Mouse came. Rat came. Squirrel, Mole, Rabbit, Polecat, and even Grizzly Bear came. *(Children can play the animals.)* They circled around the boulder and chanted as loud as they could:

> Koda and Kabato, wake up, wake up!
> Koda and Kabato, come down from the rock.
>
> *(Audience repeats these lines.)*

But Koda and Kabato did not hear them. They were still sound asleep. Each animal tried to jump up the side of the boulder, hoping to reach the top. Mouse jumped, Rat jumped, Raccoon jumped, Squirrel jumped, Mole jumped, Rabbit jumped, Polecat jumped. None of them made it to the top. Last of all Grizzly Bear tried. He jumped farther than all the other animals, but he too did not reach the top.

Tired from all the jumping, the animals had decided to go home and rest when they heard a little voice say, "I haven't tried yet." It was Tutokanula, the inchworm.

The tired animals couldn't help but smile. How could an inchworm succeed where all of them had failed? But Tutokanula paid no attention to their smiles. Step by step he crawled up the boulder until he reached the top. Once there he cried:

Koda and Kabato, wake up, wake up!
Koda and Kabato, don't sleep on the rock.

But although he was shouting at the top of his voice, Koda and Kabato kept on sleeping. Finally Tutokanula crawled on Koda's toe and began to tickle it.

That did it! Koda woke up with a start and saw with horror that he and his brother were lying on a big boulder high up in the sky. How did they get there, and how would he and Kabato be able to climb down and get back to their parents? Koda wondered.

Tutokanula crawled up to his ear, told him what had happened, and then added, "I'll teach you to climb down. If I can climb down, you can do it too."

Tutokanula's words gave Koda courage. He woke up Kabato, and they both listened very carefully as Tutokanula explained to them how to climb down a big boulder. Soon they were on their way, climbing down step by step.

When Koda and Kabato finally reached the ground, the animals cheered so loudly that the parents heard the noise and came running. *(The audience cheers.)* How happy they were when they saw Koda and Kabato. They thanked Raccoon and the other animals for their help. Afterwards they danced around Tutokanula and sang:

STORYTELLER: Tutokanula, you are so small.

AUDIENCE: You are so small.

STORYTELLER: Tutokanula, you did it all.

AUDIENCE: You did it all.
(Repeat while the children playing the animals dance around Tutokanula.)

The Rabbit and the Elephant

One day Elephant decided to ask his neighbors to help him make a farm. On the way he met Rabbit.

"A good morning to you, Elephant," said Rabbit politely.

"G'mornin', Rabbit," replied Elephant haughtily.

"May I ask where you are going?" asked Rabbit.

"I am going to ask my neighbors to help me make a farm," said Elephant.

"Oh, dear," said Rabbit. "I was going to do the same thing."

"Don't waste your time," said Elephant. "No one will come to help you. They're all coming to help me."

"Hmmmm," said Rabbit. "I think there are enough neighbors to help both of us. Maybe a few would like to help me rather than you."

"Don't talk nonsense," snorted Elephant. "Don't you know that it is an honor to help an elephant make a farm?"

Rabbit watched Elephant stomping down the road. "Elephant is getting very conceited," she muttered. "I wonder if I could teach him a little lesson."

Rabbit began to think, and suddenly she had an idea. She went home and made many hoes. Then she fastened some iron dancing rattles to them. The following day she took them to her plot of land and began to hoe. Each time she hoed, the rattles on the hoe turned and sang, "Zain, zain, zain, zain, zain, zain, zain, zain."

It sounded so nice that Rabbit made up a little song:

> Zain, zain, zain, zain,
> Hoe the ground and plant the grain.
> Pray for sun and pray for rain,
> Zain, zain, zain, zain.

> *(Audience repeats the song.)*

After a while Baboon came along. He was in a bad mood. He really didn't want to help Elephant with his farm, but he had been too afraid to say no to him. As soon as he saw the hoes with the dancing rattles and heard Rabbit's song, he stopped and said, "Rabbit, can I try your hoe?"

"Sure," replied Rabbit. She gave Baboon her hoe and got herself another one.

Soon Baboon and Rabbit were hoeing and singing:

> Zain, zain, zain, zain,
> Hoe the ground and plant the grain.
> Pray for sun and pray for rain,
> Zain, zain, zain, zain.

A bit later a big crowd of animals came. They were walking very slowly. None of them wanted to be the first to arrive at Elephant's farm. They stopped and watched by Rabbit's garden. After a while Rabbit asked where they were going.

"Elephant told us to come and help him make a farm," replied the animals. "We don't want to go, but we were afraid to say no. We would rather stay with you. Elephant is so bossy."

"Why don't you stay then?" asked Rabbit. "I have many hoes with iron dancing rattles on them."

"But what will happen if Elephant comes after us?" cried the animals.

"If we stick together and stand up to him, he might learn not to be so bossy," replied Rabbit.

"Good idea!" cried the animals. They picked up Rabbit's extra hoes and began to hoe and sing.

> Zain, zain, zain, zain,
> Hoe the ground and plant the grain.
> Pray for sun and pray for rain,
> Zain, zain, zain, zain.

Soon Elephant came stomping down the road. When he saw all his neighbors working in Rabbit's garden, he stopped in his track and gasped for breath.

"How dare you make a farm for Rabbit when I told you to help me!" shouted Elephant.

The other animals froze, but Rabbit looked Elephant straight in the eye and said courteously, "Excuse me, Elephant. Just for curiosity's sake, ask your neighbors if they really want to come and help you to make a farm."

"It's an honor to help an Elephant make a farm!" said Elephant. "Am I not the biggest and strongest animal around here? If you don't do what I tell you to do, I can stomp you all into the ground."

"First you'll have to catch us," replied Rabbit. "And second, you will never find anyone to help you make a farm if you threaten us that way. Why don't you join us, and when we are done with my farm, we will go with you and help you make your farm."

"Yes!" cried all the animals. "Come and join us and have some fun. Listen to those rattles and join our song."

"But I am —" sputtered Elephant, but no one ever heard

the rest of his sentence because Rabbit handed him a hoe. Soon he was hoeing with the rest of the animals, singing happily:

> Zain, zain, zain, zain,
> Hoe the ground and plant the grain.
> Pray for sun and pray for rain,
> Zain, zain, zain, zain.

Later on Rabbit and all the animals went and helped Elephant make his farm.

When they were done, Elephant said, "I never had such a good time in my life. I think I learned something today."

"What did you learn?" asked the animals.

"I learned that it is fun to work together in peace and harmony," replied Elephant humbly.

"Good for you!" cried the animals. And they went home feeling good.

The Day Justice Died

There once lived a peasant who owned a fine farm. He was a good and God-fearing man who worked by day and slept at night and never coveted other people's possessions.

Next to his farm lived a powerful landlord who knew nothing but his own will and who always got what he wanted. One day the landlord decided that he would like to buy the peasant's farm, raze the buildings, and use the land to enlarge the park that surrounded his mansion. He sent for the peasant and offered him a lot of money for his farm.

The peasant replied, "I love my farm. I have lived here all my life, like my father and his father before him. I intend to stay here until I die."

The landlord was convinced that money could buy him anything, so he doubled and tripled his offer. But it was no use. The peasant insisted that his farm was not for sale.

As soon as the peasant left, the landlord flew into a rage because he could not have his way. When he finally calmed down, one of his servants, a scheming wretch who was always looking for a way to better himself, approached his employer.

"Sir, there is a way to obtain the farm," he said. "All that is needed is a little cunning. I would suggest that we make a hole in the hedge that separates your park from the peasant's yard. It can be done in such a way that no one will ever notice it, except the farmer's geese who graze there."

The landlord listened to the scheme. He liked what he had heard so far.

"Sooner or later one of the geese will find the way into your park," the wicked servant continued, "and the others will follow. When that happens, you can catch them and claim that they have done great harm to your property by gobbling up rare plants and flowers. Surely you have a lawyer friend who can be bribed to support your claim, and I am convinced that you can find a judge who can settle the case in your favor."

"That is an excellent idea!" said the landlord, and he rewarded the servant with a whole handful of gold coins.

Late that night the two men put the plan into action, and just as the servant had foreseen, a week later one of the peasant's geese slipped into the landlord's park. Soon the rest of the geese followed and caused damage to the precious flowers and plants. The landlord immediately called two witnesses and a lawyer he had bribed to testify in his favor.

The following day the peasant was called before the judge. He was accused of negligence that had led to the destruction of valuable property.

The peasant, who meanwhile had found the manmade hole in the hedge, defended himself and accused the landlord of foul play. Soon, however, the peasant realized that the landlord had bribed everyone in the court. The peasant lost his farm, and of his savings, only a hundred guilders remained his own. Full of sorrow and rage, he started to leave the courtroom where he had been so wickedly cheated, but at the door he turned and said, "There is something in this world called justice, and if you misuse it, there is a greater Judge who will eventually set it right."

But the ruthless men laughed, and the judge said, "Foolish peasant! Justice died long ago, and there is nothing you or anyone else can do to resurrect it."

"If that is the truth," replied the peasant, "then the world should know it and give justice a proper burial."

The men thought it a joke and laughed even louder.

The peasant left the room and went straight to the town's bell ringer. "I will give you my last hundred guilders," the peasant said, "if you ring the death bell while I tell the people that justice has died."

The bell ringer climbed into the church tower and rang the death bell while the peasant walked slowly through the streets of the town and sang:

> Sun, dim your light. Justice has died.
> Sun, dim your light. Justice has died.

Soon the people came running and asked why he was singing such a strange song.

The peasant told them what had happened to him, and the people became very angry, for they too had been hurt by the corrupt judge and the lawyers, but they had been too scared to speak up. Now there was someone who was not afraid to fight injustice, and soon all the men, women, and children marched with him through the streets and sang:

> Sun, dim your light. Justice has died.
> Sun, dim your light. Justice has died.
>
> *(Audience sings along.)*

Soon they arrived at the king's castle. The king came outside and the peasant told him what had taken place in the courtroom.

Fortunately for the peasant and the people, the king knew the difference between justice and injustice.

He himself retried the peasant's case and became convinced that a great wrong had been committed against the peasant. "Justice was indeed dead in my city," announced the king. "But today it will be alive again." He ordered that the landlord, his wicked servant, the judge, and the lawyer receive their just punishment and saw to it that they understood the seriousness of their crime.

Meanwhile the peasant returned to his farm. The king often visited him there, because he was glad that the brave peasant had had the courage to fight for justice.

Sun, dim your light. Justice has died.
Sun, dim your light. Justice has died.

The Toy Maker

Long ago a boy was born to the great joy of his parents, who named him Uli. But when Uli was six months old, his mother realized that he was deaf. At first she was very upset, and she wondered how her son would survive in a world where most people could hear. This was long before people had developed sign language.

After a while she calmed down. "Even though our son can't hear, he already knows that we love him. If we teach him all he is able to learn, he will be fine."

The mother was right. Uli managed quite well. By the time he was twelve he had learned how to make:

(Audience joins in.)

Toy dolls who could dance,

(Pause while dolls change chairs.)

Toy bears who could growl,

(Pause while bears change chairs.)

And toy rabbits who could hop.

(Pause while rabbits change chairs.)

Every year when Christmas came around, Uli sold his wonderful toys at the annual Christmas market. People

came from near and far to buy them, because they knew
nothing would please their children more than to receive
one of Uli's

> Toy dolls who could dance,
> Toy bears who could growl,
> Or toy rabbits who could hop.
>
> *(Players change chairs.)*

Years passed and Uli's parents died, but Uli was able to
take care of himself. He had become a fine toy maker.

One day, a peddler from the city came to the little town
behind the mountains. He went to the annual Christmas
market, and his eyes lit up when he saw the

> Toy dolls who could dance,
> Toy bears who could growl,
> And toy rabbits who could hop.

The peddler went to Uli and tried to explain to him that
he would get much more money if he moved to the city and
sold his toys there. Although Uli could not hear the peddler's words, he understood perfectly well what the peddler
wanted him to do. Because he had no intention of leaving
his beloved little town, he motioned the peddler to go away.

The peddler left but he could not forget the

> Toy dolls who could dance,
> Toy bears who could growl,
> And toy rabbits who could hop.

One day, he met a fellow peddler and told him all about
Uli's wonderful toys.

After much thinking the wicked peddlers decided to
kidnap Uli and force him to make

> Toy dolls who could dance,
> Toy bears who could growl,
> And toy rabbits who could hop.

Since Uli was deaf and lived alone, it was easy to kidnap him, and one day Uli found himself in a dark basement with boarded-up windows. The two peddlers made him understand that he would be in big trouble unless he made

> Toy dolls who could dance,
> Toy bears who could growl,
> And toy rabbits who could hop.

Poor Uli was miserable. Day after day he made his toys, and the two peddlers sold them for a lot of money. But they did not prosper. They spent all their money on foolish things and forced Uli to work faster and faster to produce more

> Toy dolls who could dance,
> Toy bears who could growl,
> And toy rabbits who could hop.

One day Uli collapsed from exhaustion. Afraid that he might die in their house, the peddlers threw him out into the gutter.

Fortunately, a policeman found Uli and brought him to a hospital. The doctors and nurses took good care of him, and after a while Uli was well again. But because he could not tell anybody his name or where he came from, the people in the hospital put a mop into his hands and let him know that he was welcome to stay if he was willing to mop floors and empty trash cans.

For three long years Uli worked at the hospital. He thought he would never see his home town again. But one day Christina, a little girl from his village, needed to have an operation that only the doctors in Uli's hospital could perform. Because Christina knew that she would have to stay a long time away from home, she brought along her

> Toy doll who could dance,
> Toy bear who could growl,
> And toy rabbit who could hop.

When she put her toys on her bedside table, the doctors and nurses asked where she had found those marvelous toys. Christina told them all about Uli the toy maker, and how she had cried when he disappeared one night and was never seen again.

Just then Uli walked in to check the trash can in her room.

"Uli, Uli!" shouted Christina, and she reached out her arms to give him a hug.

The nurses and doctors were amazed when they heard that Uli was the missing toy maker who had made Christina's wonderful

> Toy doll who could dance,
> Toy bear who could growl,
> And toy rabbit who could hop.

There was great excitement in the hospital that day. Everybody came to shake Uli's hand, and Uli was as happy as he could be. But Christina was even happier because Uli was able to make her understand that he would stay with her until she was well again.

A few months later they returned to their little village, and the first thing Uli made was a small statue of a boy on his knees, praying. The villagers put the statue in their church because they knew it was Uli's way of saying thank you to God.

Turtle and Her Pesky Friends

Daniel was a lucky boy, because he lived close to a wonderful mountain lake. All he had to do on hot summer days was walk down the road, climb up the mountain, jump into the lake, and swim.

One day, Daniel found a sick turtle lying at the edge of the lake. He took the turtle home and fed it lettuce leaves. Soon the turtle felt better. It crept around in Daniel's garden and ate worms and bugs.

A few days later Turtle said to Daniel, "It's too hot here. I want to go back to the mountain lake and cool off."

"Go ahead," said Daniel. "I will follow you in a little while."

"See you later," said Turtle, and *coochatta, coochatta, coochatta (audience joins in),* Turtle crawled down the road.

After a while Turtle met Spider.

"Hello, friend Turtle," said Spider.

"Hello, friend Spider," replied Turtle.

"May I ask where you are going?" asked Spider.

"I am on my way to the mountain lake to cool off," replied Turtle.

"May I have a ride on your back?" asked Spider.

"Yes, you can," replied Turtle. "But you must promise to get off when we come to the foot of the mountain."

"I promise," said Spider. He climbed happily on Turtle's

back, and *coochatta, coochatta, coochatta,* Turtle crawled down the road with Spider on her back.

A little while later Turtle met Snake.

"A fine good morning to you, my dear friend Turtle," said Snake.

"A fine good morning to you, my dear friend Snake," replied Turtle.

"May I inquire where you are going?" Snake asked.

"I am on my way to the mountain lake to cool off," replied Turtle.

"May I have a ride on your back?" Snake hissed.

"Yes, come along," replied Turtle. "But you must promise to get off when we come to the foot of the mountain."

"I promise!" Then Snake climbed happily on Turtle's back, and *coochatta, coochatta, coochatta,* Turtle crawled down the road with Spider and Snake on her back.

Soon after, Turtle met Lizard.

"It's a pleasure to see you, friend Turtle," said Lizard.

"It's a pleasure to see you, Lizard."

"May I ask where you are going?" asked Lizard.

"I am on my way to the mountain lake to cool off," Turtle answered.

"May I have a ride on your back?" the Lizard pleaded.

"Yes, join us," replied Turtle. "But you must promise to get off when we come to the foot of the mountain."

"I promise," said Lizard. He climbed happily on Turtle's back, and *coochatta, coochatta, coochatta,* Turtle crawled down the road with Spider, Snake, and Lizard on her back.

The next animal Turtle met was Field Mouse.

"Good day to you, friend Turtle," said Field Mouse.

"Good day to you, friend Field Mouse," replied Turtle.

"May I ask where you are going?"

"I am on my way to the mountain lake to cool off."

"May I have a ride on your back?" begged Field Mouse.

"Yes, come up here!" replied Turtle. "But you must promise to get off when we come to the foot of the mountain."

"I promise," said Field Mouse. He climbed happily up on Turtle's back with all the others, and *coochatta, coochatta, coochatta,* Turtle crawled down the road with Spider, Snake, Lizard, and Field Mouse on her back.

After a long, long time Turtle came to the foot of the mountain. "We have arrived," said Turtle. "It's time for you all to get off."

"I won't," said Spider.

"Not yet," hissed Snake.

"You can't make me get off," said Lizard.

"I am not moving," said Field Mouse.

"But you promised to get off my back once we came to the foot of the mountain," cried Turtle. "I can't get to the top with you on my back."

"Ha, ha, ha," laughed Spider. "Yes, you can, old slow-poke. You are just too lazy to try."

"But I can't," wailed Turtle.

She tried to shake the pesky travelers off her back, but they held on and chided her.

> Shake, shake, shake, shake, till your shell cracks.
> You will never shake us off your back.
> *(Members of the audience get up, shake their bodies, and repeat these lines with you.)*

Turtle was very angry when she realized she couldn't shake those pesky travelers off her back. She muttered, "Who needs enemies with friends like that?" Then, feeling very disgusted, she began to climb the mountain, *coochatta, coochatta, coochatta.*

Suddenly Turtle heard steps. It was Daniel.

"Help," cried Turtle. Daniel realized immediately that Turtle had a problem getting up the mountain. He ran to her, and *coochatta, coochatta, coochatta,* Daniel pushed Turtle up the mountain.

"Hurrah," shouted Turtle, and she jumped into the water.

Off fell Field Mouse. Ka-plop!

Off fell Lizard. Splash!

Off fell Snake. Plump!

Off fell Spider. Splat!

"Help!" cried Field Mouse. "I can't swim all the way to the shore."

"I am freezing!" yelled Lizard. "This water is too cold for me."

"Get me out of here!" cried Snake. "I am not a water snake."

"There are frogs in the lake!" cried Spider. "They are trying to eat me."

"Serves you right," cried Turtle. "Remember how you treated me?"

"We are sorry," said Spider, Lizard, Snake, and Field Mouse.

"I am a slowpoke, much too slow to rescue you," replied Turtle. "Come on, Daniel, let's go have some fun."

But Daniel said, "When I say I am sorry, my dad always gives me another chance."

Turtle thought for a minute and then she said, "Your dad is right. Come and let's rescue them."

So Daniel and Turtle rescued the four pesky animals, and the animals were so thankful they never took advantage of Turtle again.

The Queen Bee

Long ago there lived a farmer who had three sons. The two older brothers were proud and selfish. The youngest brother was innocent and had a kind heart. One day the father said to his sons, "I can no longer feed you. Go out into the world and make your own living."

The three brothers rode into the world together. One day they entered a big forest. They traveled along a narrow path until they came to a big anthill.

"Why do those silly ants build their hill right in the middle of our path?" said the oldest brother.

"Ride through it," said the second brother. "I like to see them run for their eggs."

"They might crawl up your horse's legs and bite it if you try to ride through their hill," said the youngest brother. "I will take a piece of bark and push them over to the side."

"Good grief," taunted the oldest brother, "our father would be delighted if he knew that you rode out into the world to push anthills around. But do what you must do, and let's go on."

"I will," replied the youngest brother, and he moved the anthill as gently as he could to the side of the path.

By noon they came to a lake where they saw a mother duck with twelve little ducklings swimming happily about. The younger brother threw a few bread crumbs into the water, and the ducklings and their mother came up close to catch them.

"Keep on feeding them while I get a stone," said the second brother. "I want to kill that fat old duck so we can roast it for dinner."

"Don't you realize that those twelve little ducklings will die if you kill their mother?" said the youngest brother. He shooed the little creatures back to the middle of the lake where they were safe.

Greatly annoyed, the second brother scoffed, "You simpleton, we could have had a fine meal."

"An animal mother should not be harmed if she is raising little ones," replied the youngest brother. "There are laws that say so, and if someone caught you eating a roast duck at this time of the year, you could end up in jail."

"Who would catch me roasting a duck in the middle of the forest?" argued the second brother angrily. "I wish we had never taken you along." But he made no further attempt to catch the duck, and they rode on.

After a while they passed a hollow tree. A swarm of industrious bees had built a nest inside it. They had gathered so much honey that it was running down the trunk of the tree.

"Hey, look at all that honey!" said the older brother. "I would like to get my hands on that."

"Better not go too close to the tree, or the bees will sting you to death," warned the younger brother.

"What makes you think that I will stand here and wait for the bees to sting me to death?" the oldest brother said mockingly. "I will build a fire at the bottom of the tree and smoke them out before they even think of coming after me."

"Not only would you kill hundreds of bees for a bite of honey, but you might set the forest on fire," cried the youngest brother. "Look how dry everything is, and there is no water around. How would you stop a fire if it got out of hand? Forest fires spread within minutes, and you yourself might have to run for your life."

"No one needs a preacher when you are around," sneered the oldest brother. But he didn't make a fire, and they rode on.

The three brothers had hoped to pass through the forest before nightfall. It took them longer than they had anticipated, and when night came, they had no place to go. The younger brother suggested that they sleep underneath a tree. He felt comfortable in the forest and was not scared at all. But the older brothers were frightened. When the owls began to hoot, they insisted that they must find a safe place to stay.

They rode on, and after a while they arrived at an old castle. A dwarf with a long gray beard stood by the gate as if he had been waiting for them.

He asked them to come inside. The youngest brother thought it strange, but the older brothers, who were frightened of the forest, accepted the dwarf's invitation to stay inside his castle. As they entered the castle, they came into a great gray hall. Lifelike statues of young men with incredibly sad faces lined the wall. The younger brother was deeply moved by their sorrowful appearance and asked their strange host who they were. But the dwarf did not waste a look or a word of explanation on them.

Soon they entered a well-lit room. A wonderful warm meal was waiting for them. After the three brothers had eaten their fill, the dwarf led them to a bedroom. The older brothers locked the door carefully, went to bed, and snored peacefully through the night. But the younger brother didn't sleep a wink. He tossed and turned, and all through the night he heard voices weeping.

Locking the door didn't do much good. When morning came, the dwarf entered the bedroom through a hidden entrance and said to the oldest brother, "This castle and everybody in it is under a terrible enchantment. If your heart is pure and unselfish, you will have a chance to break the spell and get your just reward. If you fail, I must turn you into a stone statue."

Terrified, the oldest brother cried, "I have no intention of staying here and breaking enchantments. You can't keep me here against my will."

"You should have thought twice before you accepted my invitation," replied the dwarf coldly. "If you don't do what I say, I shall turn you into a stone statue, and you won't have a chance to try your luck. Now come on!"

The dwarf touched the oldest brother with a little gray stick, and the young man had no choice but to follow him. Soon they came to a walled-in garden, and the dwarf said, "One hundred thousand pearls are hidden in the grass. If you have not picked them up by noon, you will be turned into a stone statue."

The older brother got on his hands and knees and picked until the sweat was pouring from his brow, but when the castle clock struck twelve, he had only two hundred pearls in his bag.

The dwarf led him to the big gray hall and turned him into a stone statue. The following morning the dwarf came for the second brother, but the second brother did not fare any better than the first.

At last it was the youngest brother's turn. After he was led into the garden, he too began to search diligently for the pearls. But all the time he was searching for the pearls, tears rolled down his cheeks because he knew he would never succeed on his own and free those poor people from their terrible enchantment.

Suddenly he saw a strange sight. An army of little ants, led by their king, was coming his way. They stopped, and the king said with a squeaky little voice, "Dear friend, we have come to help you. You saved our lives, and now we will save yours."

Within a short time the ants and their king had gathered every pearl.

The younger brother was so happy that he felt like singing and dancing. He thanked his friends and gave the pearls to the dwarf when he arrived. The dwarf was very pleased.

However, picking up the pearls was only the first task. The following morning the dwarf came and took the youngest brother to a big lake.

"Twelve keys are lying at the bottom of this lake," the dwarf said. "All of them are needed to open the door to an apartment. For your sake and ours, I hope you find them."

The youngest brother plunged into the lake. When he reached the bottom, he saw that it was covered with so much mud that he didn't have a chance to find the keys. Deeply discouraged, he swam upward and sat by the lakeside.

Suddenly he saw that a mother duck and her twelve little ducklings had arrived. They looked at him with friendly eyes, and the mother duck said, "Dear friend, we have come to help you. You saved our lives, and now the time has come when we will save yours. My children will get the keys for you."

Before the youngest brother could express his gratitude, she flapped her wings and cried:

Listen, my children, listen to me.
Dive into the lake and find the twelve keys.

The ducklings disappeared under the water and returned proudly, each with a golden key in its beak.

The younger brother's heart was filled with joy. He thanked the duck and the ducklings, and when the dwarf came back, he handed him the keys.

Tears of joy came to the old dwarf's eyes, and he said happily, "You have fulfilled the first two tasks. But there is still another one, and that one is the hardest. If you complete it successfully, the spell will be broken."

The dwarf led the boy to an iron door and opened its twelve locks with the twelve keys, and they entered. In the middle of the room stood a huge bed, and on the bed slept three girls.

"These are the three daughters of the king," explained the dwarf. "You must find out which one is the youngest."

"How can I do that?" cried the youngest brother. "All three of them look exactly alike."

"The three sisters ate dessert before they fell asleep," explained the old man. "The oldest sister's dessert was sweetened with syrup. The second sister's was sweetened with sugar. The youngest one's was sweetened with honey."

"Could I go up to them and smell their breath?" asked the youngest brother hopefully.

"Unfortunately not," replied the dwarf, and he left.

The younger brother stared at the three sleeping girls and wondered how he would ever know which one was the youngest princess. All three of them looked so sweet, so sad, and vulnerable.

Suddenly he heard a buzzing noise. It was a tiny bee who was wearing a golden crown.

"I am the queen bee, from the beehive you saved, and I've come to help you," buzzed the tiny creature. "You saved my life and that of my subjects. The time has come when I can return the favor. I will sit on the lips of the princess whose dessert was sweetened with honey."

It didn't take the queen bee long to find the youngest princess. She was lying between her two older sisters, and when the old dwarf came back, the youngest brother pointed her out to him. Suddenly there was a loud crash that shook the whole castle. The younger brother closed his eyes because he thought his end had come. But it wasn't his end that had come, it was the end of the enchantment.

When he opened his eyes again, the three princesses were standing in front of him. They smiled, and the youngest one said, "Long ago, an evil enchanter gained power over us because we lived a selfish life and held nothing sacred. You broke the spell. We would be honored if you would stay and become our king."

"I'll be glad to be your king if you become my queen," said the youngest brother. And so it was decided that the youngest princess would be his bride, and they were married and lived a good and unselfish life.

And what about the stone statues? Everybody in the castle was sad about their fate, but no one thought they could do anything about it. Many years later, the youngest daughter of the king and the queen heard their story, and she started to cry. Her tears of compassion broke the second enchantment, and the statues returned to life.

What Is the Value of a Prayer?

Once there lived a good nobleman who saw to it that none of the people in his town went hungry. Every day his cook had to prepare a kettle full of good, nourishing soup and serve it to the people who were too old or too sick to care for themselves. This, of course, was greatly appreciated by the people, and they never failed to thank the nobleman and pray for the well-being of their generous friend.

One year the nobleman's fortune changed. His harvest was poor, his wife was ill, and a kinsman threatened to sue for land that rightfully belonged to him.

One day the nobleman decided to take a walk to collect his thoughts. Before long he met one of the old men who had come regularly to the castle to be fed. He greeted him by name. "How are you today, Henry?"

"Tolerable," replied the old man curtly.

"I wish I could say that about myself," sighed the nobleman. "I know you and your friends pray for my well-being. But it seems to me that you are not praying hard enough. I have so many problems."

"It's hard to pray for someone else if hunger is gnawing on one's bones," Henry replied bitterly.

"What are you talking about?" cried the nobleman.

"We are no longer receiving food from your kitchen. Because this year's harvest was poor, your steward told us that your precious supplies can no longer be wasted on old people and cripples. Naturally we assumed that he received his orders from you."

"I certainly never told him not to feed you!" said the nobleman angrily. "Go and tell all your friends to come to my castle. They will find plenty of food."

Henry thanked the nobleman and went to tell his friends the good news.

In the meantime the nobleman rushed home and called his steward before him. "How dare you cheat our poor and helpless people out of their meals, and me out of their prayers?" he shouted. "Don't you realize that I need their prayers much more than they need my food? Go instantly and see to it that they are fed and be sure to apologize to all of them."

The steward was puzzled, but he bowed and turned to leave. At the door he paused. "My lord, forgive me for asking. But I honestly wonder why you think the prayer of some old cripples are worth so much? There are more than enough priests whom you could ask to pray for you. Surely their prayers are worth more than the prayers of those beggars."

"All prayers are of great value," replied the nobleman. "Especially the ones that come from the hearts of our friends. Fortunately those prayers are free. I have the feeling that if I were asked to pay for them, I could not afford them."

"I never thought that one could measure the value of a prayer," said the steward.

"Let's find out if one can," replied the nobleman. "I know of a holy man who lives about five hundred miles from here. Go and ask him how much he thinks a prayer is worth."

"You want me to walk five hundred miles to find out how much a prayer is worth?" said the steward.

"I do," replied his master, and he sent the steward on his way.

It was not an easy journey. The steward had to cross many mountains and pass through many valleys, and when he finally arrived, he had to wait a whole month before he could talk to the holy man. People had come from near and far to seek the holy man's advice, and everyone had to wait his or her turn.

At last he was led into the presence of the old man. He asked, "How much is a prayer worth?"

"A prayer is worth a gold penny," replied the holy man.

"Is that all?" cried the steward.

"That's all," was the answer, and the steward was told to leave.

The steward traveled homeward with the answer. But when the nobleman heard it, he said, "Surely a prayer has greater value than an ordinary gold penny. Did the holy man tell you the size of the gold penny?"

"He didn't," replied the steward.

"Then you must go back and ask him," said the nobleman.

"I can't do that!" protested the steward. "I just came back from a long and difficult journey!"

"I am aware of that," said his master. "But I need to know, and therefore you must go."

The steward had no choice but to obey. The second journey was easier because it was summertime and he could sleep under the stars. But no one was happier than he when he finally was able to ask his second question. "If a prayer is worth a gold penny, how large is that gold penny?"

"As big as the world," replied the holy man.

"Couldn't you have told me that the first time?" cried the steward.

"Not unless you asked," was the answer, and once again the steward was told to leave.

When the nobleman heard the second answer, he was delighted. He put his arm around the steward's shoulders and said, "I knew all along that a prayer had a greater value than just an ordinary gold penny. A gold penny as big as the world. That sounds right to me. But I wonder . . ."

The steward turned pale, but the nobleman continued. "I wonder how thick that gold penny must be? Surely it cannot be as thin as an ordinary gold penny. I simply need to know. Steward, go and find out."

Winter was on its way, and ice and snow would soon block the roads. Would he ever return home again? the steward wondered. He said goodbye to all the folks he cared for, even to the old people whom he had called beggars in better days. They bore him no ill feelings, wished him godspeed, and promised to pray for his safe return.

The steward thanked them for their kindness and went on his way. The journey was rough. Several times the steward might not have survived if kind and generous people had not helped him. He learned what it meant to be dependent on the good will of others, and quite often he would have given his eyeteeth to have just one little bowl of soup from the nobleman's soup kettle to still his hunger.

When once again he arrived at his destination and the holy man told him that a prayer was worth a gold penny as big as the world and as thick as the distance between heaven and earth, the steward believed what the holy man was saying. All along he had felt the presence of his friends' prayers, because they had given him the strength to overcome the troubles he encountered on his third and hardest journey.

When he arrived home again, he was a different man. The nobleman was happy to hear the third answer. But he was even happier about the change in his steward. Gone were the steward's superior airs and pride. He had learned to judge people by the kindness of their hearts and not by their station in life.

What was even better, the steward and the nobleman began to pray together. Their problems did not disappear overnight, but they were able to cope with them, and needless to say, the sick and elderly and those in need received their warm and nourishing soup every day of the year.

Part Three

STORIES TO ACT OUT

The stories in Part Three can simply be told, like the stories in Parts One and Two. But these stories can also easily be acted out with children.

You may want to tell the story first. Then set up the room by following the diagram supplied for each story (See Notes on the Stories at the back of this book). Choose the children who will play each character and place them in their correct position. With a little imagination, you can create very simple props, such as a paper hat, an apron made from a towel, or a crown made from construction paper. Avoid trying to "stage" a story; it is better to let it unfold naturally and spontaneously, depending largely on the creativity the story generates.

Once the children have heard the story, they can often retell it right away. Each child has only a few sentences to speak, and they should do that in their own words. If the children have some ideas for changing or adding to the story, encourage their creativity. It is wonderful to see children bloom and enjoy themselves.

The Starling's Song

Characters:

STORYTELLER

AMOS

JOSIAH

JUDAH

REUBEN

ABIGAIL

STARLING MOTHER

STARLING CHILDREN

CAT

DOG

LION

STORYTELLER: A long time ago the Lord looked on the earth and saw that only a few of his children remembered him. Someone had to remind God's children that they had a loving Father in heaven, and since the best one to do that was his Son, God sent Jesus to this world.

On the night Jesus was born, angels appeared to an old shepherd by the name of Amos and to his young helpers, Josiah and Judah. The angels joyfully announced the good news of Jesus' birth and told the three men that they would find the Holy Child in the city of Bethlehem.

After the angels left, Josiah and Judah ran and put the sheep in their pen, while old Amos went to a shed to find a nice clean sheepskin for the baby. But while he was gone, Josiah and Judah began to worry that the long journey to

Bethlehem would be too strenuous for the old shepherd. When Amos came back, Judah said:

JUDAH: Old Amos, would you mind staying at home?

STORYTELLER: And Josiah added:

JOSIAH: We need to be back in time to let the sheep out, and if you come along, we will not make it.

STORYTELLER: Old Amos really wanted to see the Holy Child. But for a shepherd the sheep always come first. So he said:

AMOS: Go ahead, but take this sheepskin along, so the mother will have something extra to keep her baby warm. It's unusually cold tonight.

STORYTELLER: Josiah and Judah took the sheepskin and rushed off, while old Amos wrapped himself in his blanket and sat down by the fire. After a while he dozed off. He was awakened by the sound of voices. He got up and saw that his grandchildren, Reuben and Abigail, were coming across the fields. They sat down next to him and Reuben said:

REUBEN: Grandfather, Abigail and I couldn't sleep, so we came out here to keep you company. But tell us, why are the sheep fenced in, and where are Judah and Josiah?

STORYTELLER: Amos took the children's hands and said:

AMOS: Dear Reuben and dear Abigail, I have something wonderful to tell you. God's Son was born tonight. Judah and Josiah are on their way to Bethlehem to greet the Holy Child.

STORYTELLER: Reuben and Abigail were delighted, but Reuben said:

REUBEN: Grandfather, why didn't you go with Judah and Josiah to greet the Holy Child?

STORYTELLER: The grandfather smiled a bit sadly and replied:

AMOS: You know I need help when I walk nowadays, and Judah and Josiah were afraid that I would slow them down so much that they wouldn't be back in time to let the sheep out.

STORYTELLER: Reuben understood Josiah and Judah's concern, but he also could see that his grandfather would have loved to go and see the Holy Child, so he said:

REUBEN: Grandfather, Abigail and I will take you. You can lean on our shoulders, and when you get tired, we will rest.

STORYTELLER: But old Amos shook his head and said:

AMOS: Reuben, have you forgotten that my eyesight is worse than my legs? I can no longer show you the way to Bethlehem.

STORYTELLER: But Reuben smiled proudly and said:

REUBEN: Grandfather, remember that when your eyesight was still very keen, you taught Abigail and me to follow animal tracks. The moon is very bright tonight, and I am sure we can easily find the shepherd's tracks. Please say yes, for we too would like to see the Holy Child.

STORYTELLER: Seeing the eagerness in the children's eyes, Amos rose up and said:

AMOS: Let's go! Nothing would make me happier than to see the Holy Child.

STORYTELLER: Old Amos put his arms around the children's shoulders, and just as Reuben had said, they were able to see the shepherd's tracks. They walked happily towards Bethlehem. For a while Grandfather Amos felt stronger than he had felt for years. But after the first excitement had worn off, his feet began to drag. Abigail noticed it first, and she recommended that they take a little rest. Reuben and the grandfather agreed, and they all sat down under a tree.

It had been a long day, so instead of just resting, they fell sound asleep. Fortunately, a starling family that lived in the tree had also heard the good news, and those clever little birds immediately realized that the old man and the two children were on their way to see the Holy Child. But when Amos and the children didn't wake up, the starling mother said:

STARLING MOTHER: Starlings, come out of your nest and look at those sleepyheads. If we don't wake them up, they'll never make it to Bethlehem.

STORYTELLER: The starling children flew to the lower branches and sang.

STARLING CHILDREN: Tiri tirily, you won't get to see the Holy Baby.

STORYTELLER: Grandfather Amos, who was a light sleeper, woke up. When he realized what had happened, he cried:

AMOS: Children, we must have fallen asleep. Come, we must hurry.

STORYTELLER: Reuben and Abigail jumped up and grabbed hold of their grandfather, but Abigail thought that the birds might like to come along, so she said:

ABIGAIL: Thank you so much for waking us up, little birds. Why don't you come along and see the Holy Child?

STORYTELLER: The starlings were delighted with the invitation, and as they flew overhead, they began to sing:

STARLINGS: Tiri tirily, we are going to see the Holy Baby.

STORYTELLER: For a while all went well, and Reuben had no trouble finding the shepherd's tracks. But suddenly the moon disappeared behind a big dark cloud, and Reuben cried out:

REUBEN: Grandfather, it's getting too dark to see the shepherd's tracks.

STORYTELLER: The travelers stopped, and Grandfather Amos said:

AMOS: It would be nice if you had cat eyes, so you could see in the dark.

STORYTELLER: Hardly had he said those words when a cat stepped out of the darkness and said:

CAT: Meow, I can see in the dark. I can help.

STORYTELLER: But the starling mother and her children took one look at the cat and began to twitter and shriek:

STARLINGS: No, no! Go away, cat. We don't like cats. Tonight is a holy night, and we don't want to be bothered by your kind.

STORYTELLER: But the cat looked at the starling family and said:

CAT: Please do not be afraid of me. I am also on my way to Bethlehem. If you let me, I will help you.

STORYTELLER: When the starling mother heard the cat's kind words, she was embarrassed. She said:

STARLING MOTHER: I am sorry we were rude, Sister Cat. Come, we will be happy if you will show us the way.

STORYTELLER: The cat took the lead, and as Reuben and

Abigail and Grandfather Amos followed her, they once again sang with the birds.

ALL: Tiri tirily, we are going to see the Holy Baby.

STORYTELLER: But as they covered mile after mile, Grandfather Amos, without knowing it, leaned more and more heavily on the children's shoulders. Soon Abigail's shoulders were hurting so badly that she turned to Reuben and whispered:

ABIGAIL: Reuben, I didn't think Grandfather would be so heavy. How far is it to Bethlehem?

STORYTELLER: Reuben wiped his brow and whispered back:

REUBEN: We still have a long way to go. I know it's hard on you, and I wish I could find someone to relieve you.

STORYTELLER: The children didn't think anyone had overheard their whispered conversation, so they were stunned when a big dog jumped out of the darkness and barked:

DOG: Ruff, ruff, I can help. I am big and strong. Grandfather can lean on my back.

STORYTELLER: Reuben breathed a sigh of relief and was just about to accept the kind offer when the cat turned around and saw the dog. Her tail went straight up, and she hissed angrily:

CAT: Go away, dog! I don't want you to come along. Tonight is a holy night, and we don't want to be bothered.

STORYTELLER: But the dog replied:

DOG: Please do not be afraid. I am also on my way to Bethlehem, and if you let me, I will help you.

STORYTELLER: When the cat heard the dog's kind words, she said:

CAT: I am sorry I was rude to you, Brother Dog. Come along, we are glad that you are willing to help the grandfather.

STORYTELLER: The dog thanked the cat and took Abigail's place. Once again they were on their way, and as they marched along they sang:

ALL: Tiri tirily, we are going to see the Holy Baby.

STORYTELLER: Soon they reached the top of a hill and saw the town of Bethlehem in the valley. The sight was so wonderful to the grandfather's eyes that he let go of Reuben and the dog and started to run. Before he knew it, he stumbled and fell on his back. Reuben and Abigail rushed to his side and cried:

REUBEN AND ABIGAIL: Grandfather, are you hurt?

STORYTELLER: But Amos shook his head and answered:

AMOS: No, I just forgot for a moment that I am an old man. Please help me get back on my feet.

STORYTELLER: Reuben and Abigail hooked their arms under their grandfather's shoulders and tried to pull him back on his feet. But they soon realized their grandfather was too heavy for them. Reuben said:

REUBEN: I wish I could find someone to help us.

STORYTELLER: The words had barely left his mouth when a mountain lion stepped out of the darkness and said:

LION: I will be glad to help your grandfather get up.

STORYTELLER: A mountain lion? The little group was terrified. None of them realized that the lion had said he wanted to help, and all of them began to hiss, shriek, twitter, and bark.

ALL: Go away, mountain lion, go away. Tonight is a holy night, and we don't want to be bothered.

STORYTELLER: But the mountain lion said:

LION: Please don't be afraid. I am also on my way to Bethlehem, and if you let me, I will help you.

STORYTELLER: Everybody was speechless except for Grandfather Amos, who chuckled and said:

AMOS: It's taking us a long time to learn that this is a holy night. Come, Brother Lion, I'll thank you for your help.

STORYTELLER: The lion pulled Grandfather Amos to his feet, and they all walked to the city of Bethlehem. They soon found the Holy Child in the stable, and their hearts were filled with joy and adoration. After they had praised and thanked the Lord for his wonderful gift, they sat down and talked to Joseph and Mary. But after a while Abigail noticed that the baby looked very tired, and she whispered:

ABIGAIL: This baby needs to rest. He has had a lot of company. Let's sing him a lullaby.

STORYTELLER: Mary smiled thankfully, and they all began to sing as softly as they could.

ALL: Tiri tirily. Go to sleep, baby.
     Go to sleep, dear little one.
     We know that you are God's own Son.
     Tiri tirily. Go to sleep, baby.

STORYTELLER: The sweet melody put the baby to sleep, and for a while the happy but weary travelers rested with the Holy Child and his parents. But when the rooster announced the coming of the day, they tiptoed out of the stable.

As they walked home they sang jubilantly:

ALL: Tiri tirily, all of us got to see the Holy Baby.

God Is Greater Than the King

Characters:

STORYTELLER	OPALANGA
KING	OSEI'S SON
A SPY	TWO GUARDS
OSEI	NEIGHBORS

Props: A ring, a fish, and a drum

STORYTELLER: One day a powerful African king called his people together and said:

KING: You must worship me instead of God, or I'll chop off your heads.

STORYTELLER: The people were very upset, but there was nothing they could do. The king had many spies who spied on everybody all day long, and when they found someone worshiping God, they reported that person, whose head was chopped off in punishment.

One day a woman named Opalanga gave birth to a beautiful little baby boy. She handed the child to her husband, Osei, and said:

OPALANGA: Dear husband, go and carry our child up the mountain and give him a name.

STORYTELLER: Osei took his son in his strong arms. While

he carried the baby to the mountain, Osei realized that he would want his son to know about God. But what about the king and his spies? Then Osei thought of a way. He stood up, lifted the little baby toward heaven, and said:

OSEI: My son, I name you "God Is Greater Than the King."

STORYTELLER: When he came home, he put his son into Opalanga's arms and said:

OSEI: I named our son "God Is Greater Than the King."

STORYTELLER: Opalanga looked at him with horror and cried:

OPALANGA: Merciful heavens, husband Osei! What have you done? If the king hears of our baby's name, he will kill us all!

STORYTELLER: But Osei replied:

OSEI: All I can say is that I did what had to be done. The rest is up to God.

STORYTELLER: Poor Opalanga wept for days, but finally she said:

OPALANGA: Dearest Osei, I could not bear to have our son killed. Let us never call our son God Is Greater Than the King when there are people around.

STORYTELLER: Osei agreed. He and Opalanga gave the child a nickname and called him by it in front of the neighbors. But at home they called the boy God Is Greater Than the King, and when he was old enough, they explained to him why he had two names. The boy understood and grew up happily.

One evening Opalanga was feeling tired and irritable. When dinner was ready, her son was still playing with his friends. She stepped outside the door and cried:

OPALANGA: God Is Greater Than the King, come inside. Dinner is ready.

STORYTELLER: Unfortunately one of the spies heard her. He ran to the wicked king and shouted:

SPY: I heard a woman call her son "God Is Greater Than the King." Shall I arrest her and her family so you can chop their heads off?

STORYTELLER: The king shook his head and answered:

KING: No, I shall handle this differently. Go and ask the father to come see me.

STORYTELLER: The spy ran to Osei and shouted:

SPY: The king wants to see you immediately.

STORYTELLER: As soon as the spy left, Opalanga began to cry:

OPALANGA: Oh, Osei, what will happen to us?

STORYTELLER: Osei answered:

OSEI: Opalanga, I am not afraid of the king. Whatever happens, we are in God's hands.

STORYTELLER: With dignity Osei walked to the castle. But when he was led before the king, the king did not order his head chopped off. He pulled a ring from his finger and said graciously:

KING: Osei, I have heard that you are a wise man, and I want you to be my counselor. As a sign of my trust, and so the people of the city will know that you are my friend, I want you wear this ring.

STORYTELLER: Osei couldn't believe his ears. He ran home, showed Opalanga the ring, and cried:

OSEI: Opalanga, listen to this. The king wants me to be his friend and counselor, and as a sign of his trust and friendship he gave me this ring. Maybe things are changing, and a better time will come for all of us.

STORYTELLER: But Opalanga shook her head and said:

OPALANGA: Osei, do not trust the king. He is evil. He'll tell his spies to rob the ring from you and then punish you for losing it. Hide the ring in a hole underneath our sleeping mat during workdays and wear it only on feast days when you are surrounded by friends.

STORYTELLER: Osei did as his wife suggested. But a few weeks later he had to leave home for a short time. The spy, who by the king's command had been spying on Osei day and night, reported that he had left and that he wasn't wearing the king's ring. The king cried:

KING: Ha! My time for revenge has come. Go and tell the woman Opalanga to come before me.

STORYTELLER: The spy ran to Opalanga and said:

SPY: The king wants to see you right now.

STORYTELLER: Opalanga was terrified, but when she came before the king, he was again very gracious and said:

KING: Opalanga, go home and get me the ring I gave to your husband. I am going to have a duplicate made, which I shall wear at all times so the people will know that Osei is my friend and that they must obey him as they obey me.

STORYTELLER: Opalanga ran home, dug up the ring, and returned it to the king. The king dismissed her courteously, but the minute she was gone he stepped on the balcony, threw the ring into the ocean, and said:

KING: Guards, when Osei returns, arrest him and bring him to me.

STORYTELLER: The following day Osei returned, and as he entered the city gates, the guards grabbed him and they shouted:

GUARDS: You are under arrest!

STORYTELLER: They brought Osei before the king, who smiled maliciously and said:

KING: Where is the ring I gave you? Do you think so little of my gift that you don't care to wear it? Or have you sold the ring to get some money?

STORYTELLER: But Osei replied calmly:

OSEI: No, your Majesty, I have not sold your ring. I have it at home.

STORYTELLER: The king said:

KING: You have three days to prove that what you have said is true. If you can't, I will chop off your head.

STORYTELLER: Osei rushed home, moved his sleeping mat aside, and reached into the hole to get the ring. At that moment Opalanga returned from her garden and cried:

OPALANGA: Osei, what are you doing?

STORYTELLER: Osei replied:

OSEI: I am looking for the ring.

STORYTELLER: Opalanga began to look scared. She said:

OPALANGA: Osei, while you were gone, the king asked me to bring him the ring. He said he wanted to have a duplicate made and wear it at all times so the people would know that you are friends.

STORYTELLER: Osei put his arms around his wife and said:

OSEI: Opalanga, I have some bad news. The king gave me three days to come up with the ring. If I fail to do so, he will chop off my head.

STORYTELLER: Opalanga began to wail:

OPALANGA: Oh, Osei, he is doing that to you because he found out that we named our son God Is Greater Than the King! What are we going to do?

STORYTELLER: When Osei made no answer, Opalanga cried so loudly that the neighbors rushed in to see what had happened. While Opalanga was telling them all about her little son's real name, God Is Greater Than the King came running inside. He listened to his mother's words, and when she had finished her sad tale, he asked:

OSEI'S SON: But Mother, isn't God greater than the king?

STORYTELLER: Everybody gasped, but Osei lifted his son up and cried triumphantly:

OSEI: Son, God is greater than the king, and we must act accordingly. Neighbors, go home, get your drums. Opalanga and I will prepare a feast. It might be our last meal, but I want you all to come and celebrate with us that God is greater than the king.

STORYTELLER: The neighbors ran home to get their drums, and Opalanga hurried to the market and bought vegetables, meat, bread, and fish. Meanwhile Osei made a big fire, and as soon as the neighbors returned, they began to help prepare the food and roast it. But none of them felt like eating. They kept thinking about their friend's horrible fate. Suddenly Opalanga let out a scream:

OPALANGA: Osei, neighbors, look! I just opened this fish, and I found the ring.

STORYTELLER: The people crowded around her, and sure enough, there was the ring the king had given to Osei. Osei put it on his finger, and in his joy he began to dance and sing:

OSEI: It is a miracle, a miracle, a wonderful thing.
     Let us rejoice and dance and sing.
     God is greater than the king.

STORYTELLER: The neighbors thought so too. They began to beat their drums and they sang:

NEIGHBORS: We will beat our drums and sing.
     God is greater than the king.

STORYTELLER: Soon everyone was celebrating. Only the always present spy who crouched behind a tree stared in amazement. When he finally was able to gather his wits, he rushed to the king and shouted:

SPY: O King, you won't believe this! Osei and his family and neighbors are beating their drums and they are singing:

     We will beat our drums and sing.
     God is greater than the king.

STORYTELLER: The king jumped off his throne and yelled:

KING: They are mocking me. Get me my elephant. I will kill them.

STORYTELLER: The spy helped the king to mount his elephant, and he rode at great speed to Osei's house. When he arrived, the singing stopped, and the people stared at him. The king shook his fist at them and yelled:

KING: You foolish people! There is no God. Do you hear me? There is no God.

STORYTELLER: But Osei held up the ring for the king to see and said quietly:

OSEI: Who else but God would have helped me to find the ring?

STORYTELLER: Just at that moment the sun went down in the west, and one of its last rays shone upon the ring. There was a sudden flash of light. The elephant reared his front legs, and the king slid off his back. Just before he fell under the huge animal's feet, Osei jumped forward and caught the king in his arms. Deeply shaken, the king cried:

KING: Osei, why did you come to my rescue when you knew that I planned to kill you and your wife and son? Tell me, why did you save my life?

STORYTELLER: Osei looked at the king and replied quietly:

OSEI: Because I believe in God.

STORYTELLER: The king was so overwhelmed he burst into tears and asked everyone for forgiveness. Soon after, he gave up his throne, and Osei became the king and ruled his people with a humble heart.

Gold-Lillie and Spider-Millie

Characters:

STORYTELLER	OLD WOMAN
FATHER	DOG
MILLIE	CAT
LILLIE	DOLLS
BERRY BUSH	FRIENDS
WALNUT TREE	

Props: A soft dust cloth, a box with a gold-locket, and a box with a spider

STORYTELLER: There once lived a man who had two daughters. Both were nice looking, but the older girl, Millie, was mean and lazy, while Lillie, the younger, was gentle, kind, and hardworking. One day the father called the girls to his side and said:

FATHER: Millie and Lillie, I have to go on a journey. You are old enough to take care of yourselves. Share the work, take good care of the house, and be kind to one another.

STORYTELLER: Lillie and Millie assured their father they would do as he had told them, but the minute he was out of sight, Millie said:

MILLIE: Lillie, while father is gone, I am the boss. You do the cleaning, washing, and cooking, and I am going to play with my friends.

STORYTELLER: Millie's words made Lillie angry, and she protested:

LILLIE: But Millie, Father said that we should share the work.

STORYTELLER: Millie sneered and said:

MILLIE: Sharing work is not for me, sister. What Father doesn't see, he won't know. Now get busy, you silly goose, and don't you dare tell, or you will be in big trouble.

STORYTELLER: Because Lillie was much smaller than Millie, she did not have much of a choice. She sighed and went to work, while Millie ran off to play with her friends. One day Millie brought those friends home and yelled:

MILLIE: Lillie, my friends and I are going to play ball in the yard. I want you to stand behind the hedge, and whenever the ball flies over, you throw it back.

STORYTELLER: Lillie was disgusted with her sister. But again, what could she do? If Millie didn't get her way, she would make life miserable for Lillie. So while Millie and her friends played, Lillie stood and threw the ball back whenever it came over the fence. Toward the end of the game a strange thing happened. The ball came flying over the fence and bounced three times on the ground. When Lillie ran over to the spot where the ball had been bouncing, she saw a hole in the ground where there had been no hole before.

Lillie got down on her knees and peeked into the hole. Suddenly the ground gave way under her, and she fell and fell and fell. At last she landed on a beautiful meadow where the sun was shining and many flowers were blooming. Glad to be at such a lovely place, Lillie walked happily across the meadow.

After a while she came to a berry bush that was loaded

with the most delicious-looking berries she had ever seen. Because she was very thirsty, she picked a few and ate them. But when she was ready to leave, the berry bush said:

BERRY BUSH: Pick my berries, leave them not.
              If you leave them, they will rot.

STORYTELLER: Without fussing, Lillie picked all the berries and put them on a big green leaf. Wondering who would eat them, she walked on. Soon she came to a walnut tree. Lillie ate a few walnuts, but as she was about to go on, the walnut tree said:

WALNUT TREE: If you pick my walnuts, you will have a
               chance,
              To feed the wooden dolls and see them
               dance.

STORYTELLER: Lillie didn't know what the walnut tree meant by this, but she understood that the tree wanted its walnuts picked. So she picked them and cracked their shells. When she finally walked on, she left behind a big heap of ripe nut meats at the foot of the walnut tree.

At last she came to a little house. In front of it sat an old woman who smiled at her and asked where she came from.

Lillie told her story and asked the old woman if she had seen the ball. The old woman reached into her pocket, showed her the ball, and said:

OLD WOMAN: If you comb my hair, feed my dog and cat, and dust my wooden dolls, I'll be glad to give the ball back to you.

STORYTELLER: Without hesitating, Lillie ran into the house and fetched a comb. When she came back, she found that the old woman's hair was very tangled, so she took her time and tried not to hurt her as she combed it out. Afterward she looked for the cat and the dog, calling:

LILLIE: Here kitty cat, here doggie. Let me take care of you. Let me brush your fur, let me clean your bowl, let me give you some yummy food.

STORYTELLER: The dog and the cat immediately sensed that Lillie was a person who loved animals. The dog rubbed his head on Lillie's arm and barked happily:

DOG: Ruff, ruff, I like you.

STORYTELLER: And the cat purred:

CAT: Meow, meow, how do you do?

STORYTELLER: After Lillie had taken care of the dog and the cat, she found a soft cloth and began to dust the wooden dolls on the shelves in the old woman's house. Imagine her surprise when all of a sudden the dolls hopped off the shelves and began to chant:

DOLLS: If you feed us nuts and berries,
　　　　We'll dance with you, and we'll be merry.

STORYTELLER: The dolls didn't have to ask twice. Lillie ran for the nuts and berries and popped them into the dolls' tiny mouths. (*Lillie mimes this action.*) When the last berry was eaten, the dolls formed a circle and began to dance and sing.

DOLLS: Tippity tiptoe, what a treat,
　　　　To dance again on our feet.
　　　　Listen to the tip-tap sound,
　　　　As we dance and twirl around.

　　　　(*Sing to a melody.*)

STORYTELLER: Lillie joined them, and she had more fun

than she had ever had in her life. She danced and pranced and wished that the dancing would never stop. But after a while the dolls got tired and hopped back on their shelves. The old woman asked Lillie to sit next to her. She put the ball into Lillie's pocket and said:

OLD WOMAN: You are one of the kindest girls I've ever met, and I would like to give you a present. Reach under my chair, and you will find two boxes. Choose one, and hand it to me.

STORYTELLER: Lillie looked at both boxes. One was big and beautifully decorated. The other one was small and plain. Because Lillie did not want to be greedy, she chose the smaller one and handed it to the old woman, who smiled and said happily:

OLD WOMAN: You chose wisely, my dear.

STORYTELLER: The old woman opened the box, pulled out a lovely gold locket, and hung it around Lillie's neck. Because Lillie had never owned a gold locket, she was so delighted that she began to twirl and whirl around. Suddenly Lillie was back behind the fence. She heard Millie yelling:

MILLIE: Don't just stand there, Dopey, throw the ball!

STORYTELLER: For a moment Lillie thought she had been dreaming, but when she reached into her pocket the ball was there. She threw it over the fence and hurried into the house. A few minutes later Millie came inside. She began to scream at Lillie for leaving her place behind the fence, when suddenly she saw the locket. Her face turned green with envy, and she yelled:

MILLIE: Where did you get that locket? Did you steal it from one of my friends?

STORYTELLER: Lillie shook her head and told Millie what had happened. *(The audience can be asked to retell what happened.)* Of course Millie did not believe a word her sister was saying, so Lillie had to take her outside and show her the hole. When Millie saw it, she cried:

MILLIE: If you can get a locket, I can get one too.

STORYTELLER: Before Lillie could stop her, Millie jumped into the hole. Just like Lillie, she came to a lovely meadow. But when she came to the berry bush, she only stuffed herself and did not listen when the remaining berries pleaded:

BERRIES: Leave us not, leave us not.
If you leave us, we will rot.

STORYTELLER: The walnut tree fared no better. Although Millie gobbled up many of the nuts, she didn't listen when the walnut tree said:

WALNUT TREE: If you pick my walnuts, you will have a
chance
To feed the wooden dolls and see them
dance.

STORYTELLER: However, when Millie came to the old woman, she put on a pleasant face and said sweetly:

MILLIE: A very fine day to you, old lady. I am Lillie's sister Millie. Can I have a gold locket too?

STORYTELLER: The old woman looked at Millie without smiling and replied:

OLD WOMAN: If you comb my hair, feed my dog and my cat, and dust my dolls, you may have a gold locket too. *(Audience repeats these lines with the character.)*

STORYTELLER: Millie combed the old woman's hair, but she was rough and careless. (*Millie mimes this action.*) After much pulling and snatching she ran into the house and kicked the dog and cat while she slapped food into their dishes. But the dog and the cat didn't like to be treated that way. Barking and meowing, they chased Millie until she screamed for help. (*Millie screams and runs away from the dog and the cat.*) The old woman called out:

OLD WOMAN: Here kitty, here doggy, leave her alone.

STORYTELLER: Next, Millie went to dust the wooden dolls. Of all the work Millie disliked, she disliked dusting the most. (*Millie mimes this action.*) She grabbed the dust cloth and hit the dolls here and there and everywhere. As the dust flew, the dolls began to sneeze and cough.

DOLLS: Aaachoo, aaachoo, aaachoo!

STORYTELLER: The old woman didn't like the way her dolls were being treated, so she cried:

OLD WOMAN: Stop at once! I don't think it would be good for us if you stayed. Pick one of the boxes underneath my chair and leave.

STORYTELLER: Millie, of course, picked the bigger box and muttered triumphantly:

MILLIE: Ha! I'll get a bigger locket than my sister did.

STORYTELLER: But when the old woman opened the box, a big black spider jumped out and fastened itself to Millie's forehead. For a moment Millie did not realize what had happened to her, but when she reached up and felt the spider, she screamed:

MILLIE: Eeeh, eeeh! Get that spider off my forehead.

STORYTELLER: But the old woman spun Millie around, which made her head spin. Suddenly Millie was back in her own yard. There she tried desperately to pull the awful spider off her forehead. When she finally realized that it wouldn't come off, she began to scream:

MILLIE: Lillie, Lillie, help me!

STORYTELLER: Lillie and all Millie's friends came running. Lillie tried to pull the spider off Millie's head, but she couldn't. When the friends saw that the spider didn't come off, they shouted:

FRIENDS: Look at Spider-Millie.
          Doesn't she look silly?
          Ugly Spider-Millie.

STORYTELLER: Millie burst into tears and ran into the house. Lillie ran right after her and wiped away her tears. After a while Millie told her everything that had happened and cried:

MILLIE: I am ruined, I am ruined! I might as well be dead.

STORYTELLER: But Lillie said:

LILLIE: Millie, you were thoughtless and mean to everybody, but I don't think the old woman would want to ruin your life. If you tried to be a bit nicer, the spider might disappear.

STORYTELLER: Millie stared at Lillie and then asked:

MILLIE: Why are you so kind to me when everybody else is making fun of me?

STORYTELLER: Lillie gave her a hug and replied:

LILLIE: I am your sister, and I am going to help you to get rid of that spider.

STORYTELLER: Deeply touched by Lillie's love, Millie vowed she would change. It took her a while, but one fine morning she woke up and the spider was gone. The joy of both sisters was a sight to be seen. Millie never forgot that in her greatest hour of need, her despised sister had been the one who stood by her. When their father returned, he found that his daughters had become best friends and were living in peace and harmony.

Peck a Hole to Chinaland

Characters:

STORYTELLER	MRS. PETERSON
OLD WOMAN	MAYOR SIMEON
VALERIE	MRS. SIMEON
DANIEL	GOVERNOR ANDREW
FIVE CHICKENS	MRS. ANDREW
FARMER PETERSON	PRESIDENT ACHIM

STORYTELLER: One day a dark-haired old woman gave Valerie and Daniel five chickens, saying:

OLD WOMAN: Feed those chickens, and you will find new friends.

STORYTELLER: Since Valerie and Daniel liked friends, they were willing to feed the chickens. But they didn't know what chickens ate. So Valerie asked:

VALERIE: Could you please tell us what chickens eat?

STORYTELLER: The old woman answered:

OLD WOMAN: All they need to eat are June bugs and wheat.

STORYTELLER: That sounded good enough to Valerie and Daniel. They gathered June bugs from the forest and wheat from the fields and fed them to their chickens. But June passed and the June bugs disappeared. When fall came, the children couldn't find any more wheat, and Daniel and Valerie said to the chickens:

VALERIE AND DANIEL: Dear chickens, we are out of
                June bugs and wheat,
                And we don't have any money to
                buy chicken feed.

STORYTELLER: Now the chickens could have offered to lay some eggs for Daniel and Valerie to sell so they could buy some chicken feed, but they didn't. They glared at the children instead and clucked and cackled:

FIVE CHICKENS: If you don't bring us food,
            We'll eat gravel and sand
            And peck a deep hole to Chinaland.

STORYTELLER: Valerie and Daniel were amazed, and they cried:

VALERIE AND DANIEL: What! Eat gravel and sand and peck a hole to Chinaland? What will the people say? We must take you to the farmer and ask him to keep you.

STORYTELLER: So Valerie and Daniel chased the chickens to Farmer Peterson's house and both cried:

VALERIE AND DANIEL: Dear farmer, our chickens have
                nothing to eat.
                We ran out of June bugs, we ran
                out of wheat.
                They are hungry enough to eat
                gravel and sand,
                And peck a hole to Chinaland.

STORYTELLER: Farmer Peterson was amazed, and he said:

FARMER PETERSON: What! Eat gravel and sand and peck a hole to Chinaland? That's terrible. The Chinese could crawl up that hole and invade our country. Leave the chickens here. We'll find a way to feed them.

STORYTELLER: But Mrs. Peterson did not agree, and she cried:

MRS. PETERSON: Husband, think twice. We can't take in five extra chickens when we barely have enough food for our rooster and his hens. Let's help those children to chase their chickens to Mayor Simeon's house. Maybe he can help.

STORYTELLER: Farmer Peterson agreed. He and his wife helped Valerie and Daniel chase their chickens to Mayor Simeon's house. When they arrived, they all cried:

ALL: Dear Mayor, these chickens have nothing to eat.
We ran out of June bugs, we ran out of wheat.
They are hungry enough to eat gravel and sand,
And peck a hole to Chinaland.

STORYTELLER: Mayor Simeon was horrified, and he cried:

MAYOR SIMEON: What! Eat gravel and sand and peck a hole to Chinaland? We can't let that happen. We don't want the Chinese people to look up through that hole and watch what we are doing. Bring the chickens in. We'll find a way to feed them.

STORYTELLER: But his wife did not agree.

MRS. SIMEON: Husband, think twice. We can't feed five extra chickens when we have barely enough for our rooster and his hens. Let's help these people chase their chickens to Governor Andrew's mansion. Maybe he can help.

STORYTELLER: The mayor agreed. He and his wife helped Valerie and Daniel and Farmer and Mrs. Peterson chase the chickens to the governor's mansion. As soon as they arrived, they all cried:

ALL: Dear Governor, these chickens have nothing to eat.
　　We ran out of June bugs, we ran out of wheat.
　　They are hungry enough to eat gravel and sand
　　And peck a hole to Chinaland.

STORYTELLER: The governor was horrified. He said:

GOVERNOR ANDREW: What! Eat gravel and sand and peck a hole to Chinaland? That's dreadful. I have never met a Chinese person, and I have no desire to meet one. Bring those chickens in. We'll find some way to feed them.

STORYTELLER: But his wife did not agree.

MRS. ANDREW: Husband, think twice. Where will we find extra food for five chickens when we have barely enough for our rooster and his hens? Let's help these folks chase their chickens to the president. A hole to Chinaland is his problem.

STORYTELLER: Governor Andrew agreed. He and Mrs. Andrew helped Valerie and Daniel and the rest of the people chase the chickens to the White House. As soon as they arrived there, they all cried:

ALL: Dear President, these chickens have nothing to eat.
　　We ran out of June bugs, we ran out of wheat.
　　They are hungry enough to eat gravel and sand
　　And peck a hole to Chinaland.

STORYTELLER: Much to their surprise President Achim smiled and said:

PRESIDENT ACHIM: Peck a hole to Chinaland? What a wonderful idea. We could slide down to Chinaland and visit with the Chinese people.

STORYTELLER: Valerie and Daniel, Farmer and Mrs. Peterson, Mayor and Mrs. Simeon, and Governor and Mrs. Andrew were shocked. None of them knew what to say. Finally the governor asked:

GOVERNOR ANDREW: Mr. President, why on earth would you want to go to Chinaland?

STORYTELLER: The president replied:

PRESIDENT ACHIM: To make new friends.

STORYTELLER: But Valerie and Daniel asked:

VALERIE AND DANIEL: Do you think the Chinese people would like to be our friends?

STORYTELLER: The president looked at Valerie and Daniel and said earnestly:

PRESIDENT ACHIM: I hope so, because whoever seeks friends seeks peace. Now go and gather all the chickens you can find, and we will put them to work.

STORYTELLER: Valerie and Daniel gathered all the chickens they could find. As soon as there were enough, the president cried:

PRESIDENT ACHIM: None of these chickens may eat
          A grain of chicken feed.
          They may feed on nothing but gravel
             and sand,
          Till they've pecked a hole to
             Chinaland.

STORYTELLER: The chickens began to peck. They pecked

and pecked and pecked some more. They pecked till their little beaks were sore. *(All the children peck.)*

Soon there was a big hole, and the president, Valerie and Daniel, Farmer and Mrs. Peterson, Mayor and Mrs. Simeon, and Governor and Mrs. Andrew slid down to Chinaland. *(Players slide down from their chairs.)*

The first person they met was the old woman who had given Valerie and Daniel the chickens. When she saw them, she looked absolutely delighted and said:

OLD WOMAN: Welcome to Chinaland. We have been waiting for you. Come and meet new friends.

STORYTELLER: There were hundreds of people waiting for them. Valerie and Daniel and their companions bowed to them, and the Chinese people bowed back. Afterwards they talked together, they ate and drank, they sang and danced, and when the visit was over, they were sad together. But they promised to visit each other, and they have kept their promise ever since.

Bad Uncle Rat

Characters:

STORYTELLER   MISS KATZI THE CAT
MOTHER MOUSE   UNCLE DOG
SISTER MOUSE   UNCLE FOX
BROTHER MOUSE   UNCLE BEAR
UNCLE RAT

Props: A bag, a piece of cheese, and a tray of food

STORYTELLER: Once upon a time there lived a good, old mouse who had many children. Most of them were grown and doing well. Only two little mice still lived in her home. Sister Mouse and Brother Mouse were good children. They helped Mother Mouse to search for grain and seeds, and there was always enough food in the pantry.

But Mother Mouse did not only see to it that her children were well fed. Every night before they went to sleep, she talked to them about the dangers of mouse life. She said:

MOTHER MOUSE: Children, our biggest enemy is the cat. But as long as you stay away from the pantry and don't steal cheese, you will be all right. Only mice who are hooked on cheese end up in the cat's stomach. Remember that, and promise me that you will never eat cheese.

STORYTELLER: The mouse children promised, but it was

an easy promise because they had never seen or tasted cheese. The old mother mouse was an excellent example. She did not touch cheese herself, and she never, ever allowed it in her house.

One day there was a knock on the mouse family's door. Mother Mouse peeked through a crack and saw it was Uncle Rat, whom she disliked intensely. Mother Mouse wrinkled her nose, but Uncle Rat shouted jovially:

UNCLE RAT: Hello, dear Cousin Mouse. It's been such a long time since I saw you last that I decided to come and visit you.

STORYTELLER: Mother Mouse would have liked to send Uncle Rat away, but she was raised to be polite, so she opened the door and said:

MOTHER MOUSE: I guess you can come in for a spell. Sit down while I go to the pantry and find us a bite to eat.

STORYTELLER: Uncle Rat came in and sat down. But as soon as Mother Mouse was gone, Uncle Rat handed Sister Mouse and Brother Mouse a little bag and said:

UNCLE RAT: Hey, kids, I brought you something.

STORYTELLER: The Mouse children opened the bag, and inside they found some yellow lumps that smelled very good. But since they didn't know what it was, Sister Mouse asked:

SISTER MOUSE: What did you bring us, dear Uncle Rat?

STORYTELLER: Now if the uncle had said, "It's cheese," the good little mouse children would not have touched it. But all he said was:

UNCLE RAT: Eat it, you will enjoy it. I brought it as a treat.

STORYTELLER: So they ate a bite and it tasted delicious.

They were just about to take the second bite when Mother Mouse came back with a tray of goodies. When she saw her children eating cheese, she dropped the tray and screamed:

MOTHER MOUSE: You are eating cheese, you are eating cheese! Where did you get the cheese? Where did you get the cheese?

STORYTELLER: Horrified by their mother's reaction, the two little mice began to cry. And Brother Mouse sobbed:

BROTHER MOUSE: Uncle Rat gave it to us.

STORYTELLER: Mother Mouse was so furious she grabbed a broom and hit Uncle Rat with it, screaming:

MOTHER MOUSE: Get out of here, you miserable rat! Get out of here, and don't ever let me see your ugly face again!

STORYTELLER: Poor Mother Mouse got rid of Uncle Rat, but the damage was done. Sister and Brother Mouse were hooked. Although their dear mother begged them over and over again to forget the taste of cheese, they couldn't. The moon reminded them of cheese. The sun reminded them of cheese. At night they dreamed about it. During the day they whispered about it. Cheese, cheese. Cheese, cheese. Even the word *please* reminded them of cheese. At times they felt they would go crazy if they didn't get a morsel of cheese. If only the cat weren't around! But one day they overheard a conversation between old Uncle Dog and Miss Katzi the Cat. Miss Katzi said:

MISS KATZI: Friend Dog, I would like to go to my cousin's wedding, but I can't unless someone keeps an eye on the cheese. The mice and rats have been terrible this year, and I have caught dozens. But the minute I fail to catch one of those thieves, the farmer gets so angry he threatens to drown me.

STORYTELLER: Uncle Dog nodded his head and replied:

UNCLE DOG: I know what you mean. But go to the wedding and don't worry. I will keep an eye on the cheese and on the mice.

STORYTELLER: Miss Katzi thanked Uncle Dog and ran off. But as soon as she was gone, Brother Mouse grabbed Sister Mouse's hand, and they both did a little dance and sang:

SISTER MOUSE AND BROTHER MOUSE:

> The cat is gone, the cat is gone,
> And we do as we please.
> The cat is gone, the cat is gone,
> And we will eat some cheese.

STORYTELLER: Right away they snuck over to the pantry. The door was open, and Uncle Dog was lying on the threshold watching the cheese. But the mice knew that he took little naps, so they watched. When Uncle Dog began to snore, they slipped inside and began to nibble on a big yellow cheese. But Uncle Dog was just pretending to be asleep. Slowly he moved his big paws towards the silly mice. He grabbed them by their tails and yelled:

UNCLE DOG: Got you!

STORYTELLER: But the mouse tails were slick, and the mice managed to tear themselves loose. Then the race began. *(Mice and dog run twice around the block of chairs while the audience joins in the chant.)*

> Uncle Dog ran and the mice ran.
> And the mice ran and Uncle Dog ran.
> But the mice slipped into a hole.

> *(Mice crouch behind their chairs.)*

STORYTELLER: Uncle Dog was very disappointed that the mice got away from him, but he had many friends. He called for their help and yelled *(with the audience joining in)*:

UNCLE DOG: Help me, help me, help me, please,
I have to catch the mice who stole the cheese.

STORYTELLER: His plea for help was heard by Uncle Fox. Because he owed Uncle Dog a favor, he began to sniff around. *(Fox goes once around the block of chairs and sniffs while audience repeats the chant.)*

And he sniffed and he sniffed and he sniffed.

STORYTELLER: And when he found the mice, he yelled:

UNCLE FOX: Got you!

STORYTELLER: He was just about to grab them when once again they darted away. Of course Uncle Fox ran after them. *(Audience joins in.)*

Uncle Fox ran and the mice ran.
And the mice ran and Uncle Fox ran.
But the mice slipped into a hole.
(Mice crouch behind their chairs again.)

But the hole happened to be the entrance to a hollow log, and because Uncle Bear was feeding on the other side of it, the mice ran right into his arms. He had already learned that something was wrong when he heard Uncle Fox cry:

UNCLE FOX: Help me, help me, help me, please,
To catch the mice that stole the cheese.

STORYTELLER: Uncle Bear marched Brother Mouse and Sister Mouse to Uncle Fox. *(As Uncle Bear and the mice walk once around the block of chairs, he and the audience chant.)*

UNCLE BEAR: Hop, two, three, four,
                        Hop, two, three, four,
                        Hop, two, three, four, hop.
                        Hop, two, three, four,
                        Hop, two, three, four,
                        Hop, two, three, four, stop.

STORYTELLER: Uncle Fox took over and brought them to
Uncle Dog. *(As Uncle Fox and the mice walk once around
the block of chairs, he and the audience chant.)*

UNCLE FOX: Hop, two, three, four,
                      Hop, two, three, four,
                      Hop, two, three, four, hop.
                      Hop, two, three, four,
                      Hop, two, three, four,
                      Hop, two, three, four, stop.

STORYTELLER: When they arrived, Uncle Dog held onto
the tails of the mice and waited for Miss Katzi to come
back. Soon they saw her coming and heard her singing:

MISS KATZI: I had a fine time at the wedding,
                        I'm in a lovely mood.
                        I had a nice time at the wedding,
                        The food was very good.

STORYTELLER: Uncle Dog was very happy to see her. He said:

UNCLE DOG: Miss Katzi, my friends and I caught two
cheese thieves.

STORYTELLER: Miss Katzi grinned and replied:

MISS KATZI: Good, I am going to have them for dessert.

STORYTELLER: But the mouse children began to scream at the top of their voices:

SISTER MOUSE AND BROTHER MOUSE: Waaaa! Waaaa! *(Audience joins in.)*

STORYTELLER: They screamed so loud that their mother woke up from her nap. She came running and saw immediately what had happened. Although she was terrified of Miss Katzi, her love for her children was stronger than her fear. She threw herself at Miss Katzi's feet and began to wail:

MOTHER MOUSE: O dearest Miss Katzi, Miss Katzi, please,
                         Don't eat my children because they
                                 stole cheese.

STORYTELLER: Fortunately, Miss Katzi was not at all hungry that day. When she found out that Uncle Rat had lured the mice children into eating cheese, she turned to her friends and said:

MISS KATZI: Friends, you are the ones who caught these cheese thieves. What do you think I should do?

STORYTELLER: After much thinking Uncle Dog replied:

UNCLE DOG: Well, I have four small puppies, and if they did a foolish thing, I'd be happy if they had another chance. The mice children need to be punished, but maybe not so severely.

STORYTELLER: Uncle Fox and Uncle Bear nodded in agreement. Uncle Bear said:

UNCLE BEAR: Let their mother punish them, and you go and chase the wicked Uncle Rat away.

STORYTELLER: So Miss Katzi turned Brother Mouse and Sister Mouse over to their mother and went hunting for Uncle Rat. After a little while she found him. *(Audience and storyteller chant as Miss Katzi and Uncle Rat run around block of chairs.)*

> Uncle Rat ran and Miss Katzi ran,
> And Miss Katzi ran and Uncle Rat ran,
> And Uncle Rat ran and Miss Katzi ran.

Finally Uncle Rat ran off into the forest. *(Uncle Rat runs outside the room.)* When Miss Katzi came back, everybody clapped their hands and sang. *(Audience joins in.)*

> Miss Katzi is the very best cat,
> Hi hodi ho, hi hodi ho.
> She chased away mean Uncle Rat.
> Hi hodi hodi ho.

Part Four

STORIES FOR
ALL OCCASIONS

The stories in Part Four have thought-provoking themes and are good openers for group discussions about issues such as blended families, personal safety, abuse, death, and sharing. You can learn these longer stories using the method suggested in Part One. In telling these stories you may adapt some of the group-participation techniques used in Parts Two and Three.

The Christmas Quilt

Long ago there lived a merchant who had a good wife and seven nice children. One day the wife became very ill. No one could help her, and she died. Three days later they buried her in the churchyard.

As the bereaved father and his sad children walked home, they wondered how they would carry on without the children's mother. Who would care for the children and love them? They dreaded going back to their cold and empty home.

But when they entered the house, it was warm, and a pot of soup was bubbling on the kitchen stove. The children's mother's old nanny had come all the way from her village. As she hobbled toward the children, she cried, "Don't be afraid! I'll stay with you and care for you, just as I cared for your mother when she was a little girl."

The children were delighted, but their father worried that the nanny was too old for the task. He wondered if it might not be better to send her home again. But the children were so happy to be with someone who had known and loved their mother that he let her stay.

All too soon the father realized he had made a mistake.

The nanny had exhausted her strength by coming all the way from her village. Most of the time she sat behind the stove and dozed. Soon the house was dirty. The children's hair was in tangles. The baby was fretting because his little bottom was sore, and the food was either scorched or half-cooked.

Unable to stand the disorder and confusion any longer, the merchant hired a maid. The girl was cheerful and willing to work, and for a few weeks the house was clean and the food was tasty. But at the end of the month the maid came to him and cried, "I will not stay another day in this house. No matter what I do, the nanny nags. Nothing is ever good enough for her. The soup has either too much salt or too little. When I spend time with the children, she fusses and tells me that I should be weeding the garden. When I am in the garden, she yells at me for not changing the baby. No one in the world can please the old woman."

The merchant talked to the nanny, but it didn't help. Four maids came and left within six months, and the merchant was close to despair. One day a kind neighbor woman said to the merchant, "You have more problems than a man can deal with. Have you ever thought of remarrying?"

"Who would have a man with seven unkempt children and a dirty house?" replied the merchant bitterly.

"I know a young widow who loves children," said the kind woman. "I would like to introduce her to you. Who knows? Something may come of it."

Three weeks later the neighbor arranged a meeting between the merchant and the young widow. They talked for a long time, and after a while she agreed to become his wife.

The children were happy when their father told them the good news. But when the old nanny was alone with the children, she cried, "Oh, may God have mercy on you! I have never heard of a good stepmother. Don't you remember what Snow White's stepmother did to Snow White? She asked the huntsman to kill her and bring her the child's heart and liver. Then when Snow White escaped, she found her at the house of the seven dwarfs and brought her close to death by feeding her a poisoned apple.

"Cinderella's stepmother was almost as bad. She made the poor girl sit in the ashes, and she told Cinderella's father that his first wife's daughter was so dull and witless that she was better off sitting behind the stove.

"Hansel and Gretel almost lost their young lives when they were left in the woods and the witch caught them. I could tell you a thousand stories about the wickedness of stepmothers," continued the nanny. "It's just awful what those women will do!"

Needless to say, the children began to cry. They ran to their father and begged him not to remarry, but he refused to change his mind. A month later he married the young woman.

Soon the house was neat and orderly again. The children were clean. The baby was no longer sore. There were good meals on the table, and the merchant looked content.

But not the children. They stared at the stepmother with fear in their eyes, because the nanny kept on saying, "Don't trust the woman. Everyone knows that new brooms sweep well. When she gets a child of her own, envy will enter her heart. She will want your inheritance for her child, and she will turn your father's heart against you."

The young wife knew that the nanny was turning the children against her, but she didn't know what to do about it. One day she went to the same kind neighbor who had brought her and her husband together and unburdened her heart.

"What am I to do?" she said. "I am trying my best, but

all my work and all my kindness are of no avail as long as the children refuse to let me love them. I know it's the old nanny who poisons their minds with stories about terrible stepmothers. If I asked him to, my husband would send her away. But the children could not bear to lose her after they have lost their mother."

"I have an idea," replied the kind neighbor. "Christmas will be here in eight months. Let's make a Christmas quilt from the children's mother's clothes. Quilting always helps me to think, and it might do the same for you."

The stepmother agreed, and every evening when the children were sleeping, she and her kind friend worked on the quilt. They cut out a Christmas tree and put it in the center. Around it they stitched jolly elves, beautiful dolls, cuddly teddy bears, and colorful birds. But the Christmas tree itself had only three star ornaments. On those the step-mother embroidered the words *faith, love,* and *hope.* While she stitched and cut, she prayed that she would win the love of the children.

By the first day of December the quilt was finished, and the stepmother began to get ready for Christmas. She made a stocking for each child and filled it with thoughtful gifts. She baked cookies and fruitcakes for the family, and for her husband and the old nanny she concocted a delicious eggnog from a treasured old recipe.

On Christmas Eve the family went to church. Afterward the father lit the candles on their tree, and the children found their stockings. They couldn't help but enjoy the gifts, and each child shook the stepmother's hand and thanked her politely. But when at last the stepmother unrolled the Christmas quilt, the children gasped. Never had they seen such a work of beauty.

How wonderful it was to see the flowers and stars, bears

and dolls, and the big Christmas tree, all cut from their beloved mother's old aprons, scarves, and dresses. Excited, they began to talk about the past, which they had never done before in the presence of their stepmother. When they were finally in bed, the stepmother covered them with the new quilt, and all of them were happier than they had been for a long time.

Only the old nanny did not share their joy. As soon as the stepmother left the children's bedroom, she snuck inside, snatched the quilt away from the children, and cried, "Shame on you! Your mamma is crying in heaven because you gave your love to that woman." She threw the old quilt over them, stuffed the new one into a sack, and carried it up into the attic.

Two hours later, when the stepmother came into the room to check if all legs and arms were properly covered, she found the children asleep under their old quilt.

The following day nothing was said. The children sat around and tried to read and play, but their eyes were filled with sadness. So were the eyes of their stepmother. The hopes of many months had been shattered in one moment. It was the most miserable Christmas Day the family had ever had.

But all days pass, even bad ones, and when evening came, the children crept under their old quilt and fell asleep.

Only the nanny couldn't sleep that night. She had a bad conscience, but pride kept her from admitting that she had been unkind. She tossed and turned, and in the middle of the night she got up, thinking a drink of eggnog might help her sleep.

Quietly, so she would wake no one, she crept downstairs into the kitchen and poured some eggnog into her tumbler.

On the way upstairs her hands trembled, and she did not notice that she spilled half of the eggnog on the steep stairway. The following morning, when the stepmother ran downstairs to start breakfast, she slipped and fell all the way to the bottom of the stairs.

Fortunately, no bones were broken. But the stepmother had a deep gash on her forehead, and the doctor who had been called gave orders that she should sleep downstairs in the parlor until she was well again.

When the merchant found out what had caused the accident, he scolded the nanny for her carelessness.

This upset the nanny so much that she went back to bed. When the children looked in on her, they found her moaning and groaning, "It's all my fault. It's all my fault. If your stepmother dies, it's all my fault."

Seeing her cry, the children cried too, and the oldest one said, "We were foolish. We never realized that our mother would want us to have a good stepmother. How can we show her that we love her?"

"I know what we can do," cried one of the boys. A little while later seven young children tiptoed into the parlor and covered their stepmother with the Christmas quilt.

During the following days the children and their father surrounded the stepmother with so much loving care that she was soon up again. But the nanny would not get out of bed. She insisted she was a burden to everybody and that her time to die had come. She probably would have died, except for the stepmother, who went to her room. "You must not think of dying," she said. "The children love you and need you to talk about their mother."

"They do?" asked the nanny with a trembling voice.

"They do," replied the stepmother, "and I need you to help me with the mothering."

"May God bless you for those words," sobbed the nanny. "I had a cruel stepmother, and I did not want the children to love you, because I was afraid they would be disappointed."

"You tried to do what you thought was good for them," replied the stepmother. "But let's help each other and always remember the words I embroidered on the three Christmas stars."

"Faith, hope, love—these three abide," whispered the nanny. "But the greatest of these is love." And so it was.

Budulinek

A boy named Budulinek lived with his grandmother in a little hut near a big forest. Granny had to go to work every day, and when Budulinek was small, she paid a kind neighbor to watch him. But on Budulinek's fifth birthday she said, "Do you think you could stay by yourself while I'm at work? We could save the money we would have given the neighbor and buy you a pair of new shoes."

"Of course," said Budulinek. "I can stay by myself. I am a big boy now, and I want to have a pair of new shoes."

Granny was glad to hear that, and the next morning she said, "Budulinek, there is some leftover soup. Don't eat it before noon, and don't open the door to strangers."

"I won't," replied Budulinek, and he locked the door behind her.

Budulinek played, and when noon came, he took his soup and sat on the windowsill to eat it. Suddenly he heard a voice saying, "Budulinek, can I come in and keep you company?"

Budulinek looked up and saw a fox in the little garden behind his hut.

"Go away," said Budulinek. "I can't open the door to a stranger."

"Budulinek," laughed the fox, "you know I'm not a stranger. I'm just a lonesome fox, and if you open that door for me, I'll give you a ride on my back. It will be so much fun. We'll be running down the road, and the wind will blow through your hair, and the children will say, 'Look, look, there goes Budulinek. He is riding on the back of a fox.'"

But Budulinek remembered his Granny's words, and he replied, "Didn't you hear what I said? Go away! I'm not supposed to open the door to strangers."

But the fox didn't go away. He kept on talking about giving the boy a ride on his back until Budulinek couldn't stand it any longer and let the fox in.

Did the fox give him a ride on his back? He didn't! He gobbled up Budulinek's soup, and lickety-split, just like that, he ran out again.

When Granny came home that night, Budulinek looked very sad, and his stomach was growling, "Rumble, rumble, rumble." *(Audience joins in.)*

"What's that noise?" asked Granny.

"It's my stomach," said Budulinek, and he began to cry, "Waaaa, waaaa, waaaa." *(Audience joins in.)*

"Didn't you eat your soup?" Granny asked.

"No, I didn't. The fox ate it," replied Budulinek.

"You opened the door for the fox?"

"He—he—he promised me a ride on his back," sobbed Budulinek.

"You promised me not to open the door to anyone," cried Granny, greatly upset, and she punished Budulinek. But afterwards she hugged him and said, "Now do you know why I tell you not to open the door to strangers? They might steal things, and they might steal you. Please promise not to open the door to anyone."

Budulinek promised, and they ate dinner and went to bed.

The next morning Granny said, "Budulinek, I have been thinking. I had better take you to the neighbor."

"No!" cried Budulinek. "I won't open the door again. Please, Granny, trust me."

"All right," said Granny. "There are some leftover dumplings. Don't eat them before noon, and remember what I said about the door."

"I will," said Budulinek, and he locked the door behind her.

Lunchtime came, and when Budulinek took his dumplings and sat on the windowsill to eat them, he heard that voice again. "Budulinek, can I come in and keep you company?" *(Audience joins in.)*

Budulinek took one look at the fox and yelled, "Get out of my garden or I am going to take a bucket full of water and pour it over your back."

The fox pleaded, "Don't be angry at me, Budulinek. I ran away yesterday because my oldest son had fallen into a big hole, and I had to pull him out. I came back to apologize and to give you a ride on my back. Come on, Budulinek, you will have so much fun. We'll be running down the road, and the wind will blow through your hair, and all the little children will shout, 'Look, look, there goes Budulinek. He is riding on the back of a fox.'" *(Audience joins in.)*

Budulinek sighed. Was the fox telling the truth? Maybe he was. Why else would he have come back? For the second time Budulinek forgot his promise. He went to the door and opened it. In came the fox. He gobbled up the dumplings and left.

This time Budulinek was really angry. He ran after the fox and screamed at the top of his voice, "Come back, you rascal. You scoundrel, you villain, you liar!" But the fox did not come back.

When Granny came home that night, she heard that strange noise again. "Rumble, rumble, rumble." *(Audi-*

ence joins in.) Budulinek could not keep his stomach from grumbling, and once again Granny found out what had happened.

"You opened the door a second time," she cried, and tears gathered in her eyes.

Budulinek was terribly embarrassed, and when Granny punished him again, he felt he deserved it. When she hugged him afterwards and told him that she loved him so much she could not bear to lose him, he cried and promised that he would never open the door to the fox or anybody else again.

The third day came, and Granny did not mention the neighbor because she was convinced Budulinek had learned his lesson. She fixed him a sandwich, and when noon came, Budulinek took it to the windowsill and wondered if the fox would have the nerve to come back.

The fox did come back, and before Budulinek could say a thing, he cried, "Budulinek, I don't expect you to believe what happened. But my second son fell into the river, and I had to run and pull him out or he would have drowned. Will you forgive me for not keeping my promise?"

"I won't," said Budulinek coldly. "I think you are the biggest liar in the world. Go away and don't ever let me see you again."

"This time you will get a ride on my back," cried the fox. "Mrs. Fox is keeping the children in our den, and nothing will happen to spoil our fun. We will be running down the road, and the wind will blow through your hair and all the children will shout, 'Look, look, there goes Budulinek. He's riding on the back of a fox.'" *(Audience joins in.)*

"And no one," added the fox, "has ever been offered a ride on the back of a fox but you, Budulinek. Come on! This is your last chance."

"My last chance," thought Budulinek. "Maybe the fox really means it." Once again Budulinek forgot his promises. He opened the door, and the fox came in. He gobbled up Budulinek's lunch, but before Budulinek could scream at him, he said, "Climb on my back, boy."

"This time he is keeping his promise," thought Budulinek. He climbed on the fox's back, and the fox ran out of the house. But he didn't run down the road, he ran into the forest.

"No, no," cried Budulinek. "I don't want to go into the forest."

"Hush your mouth," sneered the fox, and he ran to his den and pushed Budulinek inside. Poor Budulinek. He tried, but he couldn't get out again. Mr. Fox and Mrs. Fox blocked the entrance, and they laughed when the little foxes jumped all over Budulinek and tore his shirt and scratched his face. When Budulinek opened his mouth and started to cry, they thought he was hungry, and they put a dead mouse into his mouth. Yeeeech! Budulinek was very unhappy.

When Granny returned to the little hut that night, the door was open, the chair was overturned, and the plate was on the floor.

"Budulinek," cried Granny. "Budulinek, my little Budulinek, where are you?"

No one answered.

Granny searched the hut. She searched through the garden. She ran out into the street and cried, "Budulinek, my dear Budulinek, where are you? Where are you?" She asked the neighbors. *(Ask members of the audience.)* But they didn't know.

Only one little boy said, "I think I saw him riding on the back of a fox. But I don't know where they went."

"Riding on the back of a fox," whispered Granny,

horror-stricken. "Oh, may God help me! If he was riding on the back of a fox, I'll never get him back." She began to cry bitterly. *(Cry, so the children will see real grief.)*

Trying to comfort her, the neighbors said, "Budulinek will come back. The fox can't keep him forever."

Granny couldn't believe it. She sobbed, "It's all my fault. I should have asked my dear neighbor to watch him. But I wanted to save the money to buy new shoes, and now my Budulinek is gone."

While she was crying, a forester came along and asked what was wrong.

After the people told him what had happened, he said, "Go to bed, Granny. It's too late to find Budulinek tonight. But early tomorrow morning I'll go into the forest and look for him. I have never heard of a fox eating a boy."

Granny stopped crying and followed the advice of the forester. Although she knew she wouldn't be able to sleep a wink, at least she could hope and pray.

Early the next morning the forester kept his promise and went into the forest to look for Budulinek. He walked quietly among the trees. After a while he heard a muffled voice crying, "Let me out of here! Let me out of here!"

"Aha!" said the forester. "There he is." He followed the voice, and it led him straight to the fox's den. Without making a sound, the forester took some dry branches and made a tiny fire next to the opening. He knew that all forest animals run when they smell smoke. As the smoke drifted into the den, the fox rushed out to see what was going on, and he ran right into the forester's knapsack.

The forester put the fire out, and then he shook the knapsack with the fox in it and said, "If you dare to steal another boy, I will come back and put you into the zoo, and you will never see your wife and children again."

The fox begged for mercy and promised, and the forester set him free.

Then the forester pulled Budulinek out of the fox's den and took him home. Granny hugged him and kissed him, and she did not punish him, because she could see he had suffered enough.

The Shipwrecked Merchant

Once upon a time Aaron, a God-fearing merchant, decided to travel across the ocean and sell his wares in foreign lands. A terrible storm wrecked the ship he was on, and all the passengers drowned except Aaron.

For days he drifted on the sea, supported by nothing but a piece of wood, until the waves carried him to an island. He crawled onto the beach and saw a big city. A group of people stood in front of the city gate. When they saw him, they ran toward him, shouting joyfully, "There is our king. There is our king."

Before Aaron could explain who he was and where he came from, the people helped him to his feet, put a purple robe around his shoulders, and led him to their city. As they entered the gates, bells began to ring, and hundreds of people came out of their houses. They sang and danced, tossed flowers, and shouted, "A good life to our king! A good life to our king!"

Soon they came to a splendid castle. The people took Aaron inside and had him sit on a golden throne. A priest came to anoint him, and six noblemen crowned him with a golden crown. Having just escaped death, Aaron was amazed at what was happening to him. He felt he could not trust his eyes or his ears. In fact, he thought it was all a strange dream and he would soon wake up and find himself lying on the beach.

Evening came, and he went to sleep. But when he woke up the following morning, nothing had changed. Servants came. They washed him, dressed him, and served him breakfast. During the morning hours, ministers and counselors arrived and briefed him on state affairs. Military officers came with reports about the army, and when at the end of the morning the treasurer handed him the key to the treasury, Aaron began to believe that they indeed wanted him to be their king.

During the following weeks and months, Aaron tried to be a good king. He saw to it that justice was done. He shared the wealth of the treasury with the poor, and because he did not believe that anyone should be the slave of another, he set all the slaves free.

In gratitude the former slaves went out of their way to please the new king.

Late one night, after Aaron had finished his many duties and was praying, he sensed that someone was watching him. He looked up and saw that one of his servants was gazing at him with tears in his eyes. Once again Aaron began to wonder about his strange fate. When morning came, he called the servant to his side and said, "I have lived here for six months, and I have not been able to find out why the people chose me to be their king. Why do they entrust their lives and fortunes to me and allow me to rule them? I am sure that you know, and I beg you to tell me why this is happening to me."

The servant, who formerly was a slave, replied sadly, "My king, it is a secret that I am forbidden to reveal."

"I cannot go on without knowing," Aaron said. "I have made up my mind that I will neither eat nor drink until I know the truth."

The poor servant, who loved the king with all his heart,

begged him to give him time to think. A few days later he came to the king and said, "I have decided to reveal the truth to you. For many years it has been the custom on this island to choose a stranger to be our king. Every year on the first day in May, our elders wait in front of the gates, and the first person who comes along is chosen to be our king for twelve months. But as soon as the last day of April comes, his royal robes are removed, and his old clothes are given back to him. Then he is led to the seashore. Two sailors put him into a small boat and take him to a deserted island, where he is abandoned to his fate."

When the king heard those words, he was amazed. He asked, "Didn't the other kings ever ask questions?"

"They did," replied the slave. "But they were told not to worry. In time they accepted their good fortune. They lived in splendor and cared only for their own well-being. You are the only one who made life better for the slaves and insisted on knowing why you were chosen to be our king."

"Tell me what I should do," said Aaron.

"If I were you," replied the servant, "I would secretly prepare the island for your arrival. I would send faithful servants to break up the soil and plant grain. I would ask them to take chickens, ducks, geese, sheep, and cows to the place and have them build shelters for people and beasts. By the time you arrive, the island would be ready for habitation."

The servant's advice pleased the king. With the servant's help, the king selected the most trustworthy servants and sent them secretly to the island. There they built shelters, plowed the soil, and planted seeds. When the last day of April arrived, everything happened as the servant had said. The counselors, vassals, officers, and ministers acted as if they had never seen the king before. Servants came and took away the key to the treasury, pulled off his clothes, and handed him the old clothes he had worn when he arrived.

They led him through the city to the beach and put him into a small boat. Two sailors brought him to a deserted island and left him on the rocky shore.

Little did they know that beyond the cliffs was a well-prepared home for Aaron and the faithful friends who were waiting for him. With them he lived in peace and harmony for the rest of his life.

Small Fry

Small Fry lived in a pond at the foot of a great mountain. The dark green waters made it impossible for his school of fish to see anything except the watery world in which they lived. All day Small Fry and the other fish swam in circles, round and round, each fish moving at the same time, each in the same direction.

Frog lived in the pond too. Although he was not a fish, he liked talking to any fish who would listen.

Small Fry and Frog became friends. They spent many hours together chatting about first one thing, then another. Frog did most of the talking. Small Fry listened. Frog told strange stories about wonderful creatures that flew in the air and large creatures that walked on land.

Like all the other pond fish, Small Fry believed there was nothing beyond the pond. In fact, he didn't believe in land, sky, trees, or flowers. He thought that when Frog disappeared, he was just hiding in another part of the pond.

"You don't believe a word I've been telling you," said Frog.

Small Fry blushed. "Well, not exactly. The wise fish tell us there is nothing beyond the pond."

"Nonsense," said the Frog. "And I'll prove it to you, if you're brave enough to try."

Small Fry thought for a moment. He knew the wise

ones would not approve. He had been warned never to listen to any of Frog's stories. But what if there were something beyond the pond? Small Fry wanted to know. "I am brave enough to try," said the little fish.

"Good," answered Frog. "Come to the water's surface in the morning, and I will have the Great Bird of the Mountain take you for a sightseeing tour of the World Beyond the Pond." Frog croaked and then disappeared.

Small Fry could hardly sleep. Who was the Great Bird of the Mountain? Would he be a terrible monster? When the dark waters lightened, Small Fry slowly swam to the surface. He was so afraid. Suddenly he felt himself being lifted out of the water by a powerful force.

"You must be the Great Bird of the Mountain," said Small Fry.

"Yes," said the large bird. "Don't be afraid. Frog asked me to take you on a sightseeing tour of the World Beyond the Pond. We haven't much time, so let's get started."

Small Fry rested in the bird's great talons. As the bird's wings flapped back and forward, they moved higher and higher. Small Fry could see the pond far below. It was very small. He saw Frog sitting on a lilypad in the center of the pond. Small Fry saw trees and flowers for the first time. They were just as Frog described them. As the Great Bird flew higher, Small Fry saw bears, bees, rabbits, mice, and squirrels. There *was* a world beyond the pond!

Then, too soon, it was time to go back to the pond. "Fish can't stay out of water too long," said the Great Bird. Slowly he glided toward the pond and gently released Small Fry into the water.

The little fish was so excited about his adventure he could hardly wait to tell the others in his school.

"I wouldn't do that," Frog warned.

But it was too late. Nothing could stop Small Fry. "There is a world beyond the pond," he shouted joyfully. "There are creatures who walk on land, and creatures who fly in the air."

All the fish laughed. "You are a silly fish telling a silly story," said one of the other fish.

"But I saw these things with my own eyes," Small Fry argued.

"Who told you about a world beyond the pond? There is no such place," said the oldest of the fish.

"But it is so! I saw them," said Small Fry. "I was taken for a sightseeing tour of the World Beyond the Pond by the Great Bird of the Mountain," he answered.

"Stop," cried the leader of the fish school. "Enough of this!" The fish moved away from Small Fry. "You had a bad dream, or you are mad," said the Leader Fish. "You have been listening to Frog's stories too much. I forbid you to talk to Frog ever again. I demand that you never discuss any of this madness with the other fish. Otherwise I will be forced to ask you to leave us. Do you agree?"

"But . . . ," said Small Fry. "Yes," he said at last. "I agree."

But whenever he could, Small Fry swam to the water's surface. He swam in circles, making them wider and wider, building speed. Then he leaped from the water as high as he could. High in the air, he could see flowers and trees, bees and bears, rabbits and squirrels. He saw his friend Frog resting on his lilypad and the Great Bird of the Mountain who often came to the pond to drink. For a brief moment Small Fry could enjoy the World Beyond the Pond.

Kind Ivan

There once lived a young man named Ivan whose mother loved to decorate Easter eggs. But she did not keep the eggs for her family. She gave the eggs to all her friends and neighbors, because people in Russia are especially kind to each other at Easter time.

One year one of her eggs was so beautiful that she decided to give it to the tsar. Because she was too old to travel, she called her son and said, "Ivan, please take this egg to the tsar. But while you are traveling on the roads of Russia, remember that it is Easter time and that we must be especially kind to all the people who cross our path."

Ivan promised to remember, and he traveled to the tsar's city. When he handed the egg to the tsar, the tsar was so delighted that he gave Ivan a golden egg in return. Ivan thanked him for his kindness and traveled homeward.

Soon a horseman overtook Ivan. They began to talk to each other, and Ivan told the horseman about the golden egg.

"You are a lucky man," said the horseman. "If someone would give me an egg like that, I would never wish for anything else."

Ivan would have liked to keep the egg, but he remembered his mother's words, so he said, "If it will make you happy, I'll give it to you."

"If that's what you want to do, I will not stop you," cried

the horseman. "But because it's Easter time and you are so kind to me, I will be kind to you too. Here, take my horse in return."

"I'll be glad to take your horse," said Ivan, and he jumped on the horse's back. But the horse took off like lightning, and Ivan fell off and landed in a ditch.

Fortunately, a farmer who was walking a cow to market stopped the horse and helped Ivan get back on his feet.

"You must not be used to horses," said the farmer.

"You are right, I am not," replied Ivan, and he told the farmer how he came to have the horse.

"It's a nice horse," said the farmer. "I would be happy to have one like it."

Ivan remembered his mother's words and he said, "I'll be glad to give you the horse."

"If that's what you want to do, I will not stop you," cried the farmer. *(Audience repeats this line.)*

"But because it's Easter time and you are so kind to me, I will be kind to you. Here, take my cow in return."

"I'll be glad to take your cow," said Ivan. And he took the cow and walked down the road.

After a while he became very thirsty. "I will milk some milk into my hat and suffer no longer," thought Ivan. He sat by the wayside and began to milk the cow.

Not a single drop of milk came forth. Just then an old woman with a fat pig came along and asked, "Are you having a problem, young man?"

"There is not a drop of milk in this cow," cried Ivan.

"She is a fine milk cow," said the old woman. "But she will have to calve before she will give milk. I wish I had a cow like that."

Now Ivan would have liked to take the cow home, but once again he remembered what his mother had told him and he said, "If it makes you happy, I'll give the cow to you."

"If that's what you want to do, I will not stop you," cried the old woman. *(Audience repeats this with you.)* "But since you are nice to me, I will be nice to you and give you my pig in exchange."

Ivan walked on, feeling good about himself. But the pig was stubborn. It ran from one side of the street to the other, and suddenly it hopped into a gutter by the roadside and began to wallow in the mud.

While Ivan was struggling to get it out, a young woman by the name of Marushka came along. She was on her way to the market to sell a basket of eggs. When she saw Ivan grappling with the pig, she put down her basket and helped him to pull the pig out of the mud.

The minute the pig was back on the road, it ran to the basket and turned it over. All but one of the eggs were broken.

When Marushka saw the damage, her eyes filled with tears, and she said, "I was going to sell the eggs and buy my mother a scarf for Easter."

"Please don't cry," said Ivan. "I'll give you the pig in exchange for the egg."

"If that's what you want to do, I will not stop you," cried Marushka happily. *(Audience repeats this with you.)* She threw her arms around Ivan's neck and gave him a hug. Together they drove the pig to her house and then bade each other farewell.

"I made many people happy," said Ivan to himself. He went home to his mother and told her everything that had happened.

His mother smiled and said, "Ivan, you have a good heart. Let me see what I can do with the egg."

She went into the kitchen, boiled the egg, and decorated

it with flowers and hearts. On Easter day she asked Ivan to take it to Marushka.

Marushka was very happy about the egg, and the next Sunday she went to visit Ivan's mother to thank her. The two women liked each other right away. They began to visit back and forth, and Ivan's mother began to teach Marushka how to decorate Easter eggs.

Ivan smiled a lot during those days, and a few weeks later he said to his mother, "How would you like it if I took a wife?"

"If that's what you want to do, I will not stop you," said Ivan's mother. *(Audience repeats this line with you.)*

Ivan ran and asked Marushka to marry him. Marushka said yes, and they set the date for the wedding.

On his wedding day Ivan's guests asked Ivan how he had met Marushka. Ivan told them about the tsar's egg, the horse, the cow, the pig, and Marushka.

Some of his guests laughed and said, "Ivan, you were silly. If you had kept the tsar's egg, you would be rich now."

"Maybe, and maybe not," replied Ivan. "My mother told me that at Easter time we should be kind to all the people who cross our path. If I had kept the tsar's egg, I would not have met Marushka and learned how kind she is. And is not kindness more valuable than a hundred golden eggs from the tsar?"

> What do you think? Let me know by tonight,
> Was Ivan wrong, or was he right?

The King and the Abbot

There once lived a king who ruled over a small country, but being a ruler did not give him much pleasure. Because his neighbors were powerful and greedy kings who plotted to snatch away his land, he constantly had to ride to his borders to see that they were well guarded.

One day, on his way to yet another trouble spot, the king passed an abbey. Tired and hungry, he asked for some food for himself and his men. The abbot served the finest food and wine and did his best to make the king comfortable.

As they were dining, the king began to think how he soon would have to leave and spend hours on the back of his horse, eating nothing but bread and sausage, while the abbot was living in comfort and splendor.

"It's a dog's life I lead," muttered the king to himself, and he decided to make life a bit harder for the abbot.

At the end of the meal he said sternly, "Abbot, for a man of God you live too comfortable a life. I am afraid that this may lead to overindulgence, and I have decided to save you from that sin. I expect to be back in my castle within three months, and by that time I want you to give me an answer to three questions.

"When you come to see me, I will be sitting on my golden throne. I will be wearing my velvet robe trimmed with ermine, and I will be holding my golden scepter in my hand. My golden crown, studded with costly jewels, will be on my head, and a golden chain with the royal seal attached to it will be hanging around my neck.

"I am sure, my dear abbot, that a man who manages to live a more comfortable life than a king will have no trouble answering my first question: How much am I worth in pennies and guilders when I am in my royal robes?"

The abbot looked horrified, but the king continued. "I am sure the second question will also be easy for a brilliant scholar like you to answer. I have always wanted to know the answer to this question: What would be the fastest way for a man to ride around the world?"

"Your Majesty," stammered the abbot, "these questions are impossible to answer."

"Are they?" laughed the king. "Wait until you hear the third one. When you stand before me, surrounded by all the noblemen of this country, I will say to you, 'Abbot, What am I thinking at this moment?' And you had better come up with an answer."

Before the abbot could say another word, the king jumped up, thanked him for his hospitality, and walked out the door.

After the king had mounted his horse, he turned and cried, "Abbot, if you can't come up with the answers, you will no longer be the abbot of this fine abbey. You will be put backwards on a donkey and you will ride that way through the whole kingdom."

The abbot thought for a whole week, but at the end of the week he wasn't any wiser. The second week passed, and he was so exhausted from thinking that he began to lose weight. During the third week nightmares began to haunt him. He saw himself riding backwards on a donkey, and all the little children of the country dancing around him, singing:

> Here he comes an abbot who doesn't know a
> thing.
> He cannot even answer the questions of the king.

During the fourth week the abbot sent messengers to all the schools and universities in the country. A big reward was offered to anyone who could help him find the answers for the king, but no one could. When the messengers came back empty-handed, the abbot began to waste away. He paced the floor day in, day out, and he did not know what to do.

One day he decided to take a long walk. On the way he met his old friend, the shepherd Hans. The shepherd stared at the abbot. "God help you, Your Eminence, you are almost as lean as I am," said the shepherd. "What in the world has happened to you?"

The abbot sighed deeply and replied, "I have lost a lot of weight from worrying. Three weeks from now I have to appear before the king, and I must have the answer to three questions. If I don't, not only will I lose my abbey but I will be put backwards on the back of a donkey, and they will make me ride through the whole kingdom."

"That sounds gruesome to me," said the shepherd. "Tell me the king's questions. Maybe I can help. I don't know how to read or write, nor do I know a word in Latin and Greek, but I inherited something from my mother. They call it mother's wit around here. Maybe it will come in handy."

"Oh, Hans," cried the abbot, "if you find an answer to the king's questions, you will never want for a thing in your life. Listen to me. These are the king's questions." *(Give the audience a chance to recall the questions.)*

1. How much is the king worth in his royal robes?
2. What is the fastest way for a man to ride around the world?
3. What is the king thinking at the moment when the abbot is standing before him?

After the shepherd had heard the questions, he said, "I think I can help you, but only under one condition. I will have to go dressed as the abbot, and you must stay here and be the shepherd Hans. It's a good thing that you have lost a lot of weight or else we would not be able to do this."

"I will do anything," agreed the abbot. "But you must teach me how to take care of the sheep."

"I also must learn," replied the shepherd. "If you teach me to conduct myself like an abbot, we both will be all right."

At the end of the three months the shepherd traveled to the king's castle as the abbot, and the abbot stayed home to care for the sheep.

When Hans, dressed as the abbot, arrived, he was led to a huge hall filled with noblemen and noblewomen who wanted to hear the answer to the king's questions. The king himself, dressed in all his royal splendor, was sitting on his golden throne. When Hans stepped before him, the king said, "Welcome my friend. Rumors tell me that my questions bothered you so much that you have lost a lot of weight."

"It will be better for my health," replied Hans quietly.

"It will also be better for the back of the donkey if you fail to answer my questions," said the king. "Now go ahead and give me an answer to my first question: How much am I worth in my royal robes?"

"Twenty-nine silver pieces," replied Hans.

"You don't think I am worth very much," said the king. "How did you come up with that number?"

"Judas Iscariot received thirty silver pieces for betraying Jesus. Would you expect to be worth more than the Lord?"

"Indeed, I wouldn't," replied the king. "My dear abbot, that was an excellent answer. It teaches me never to become too conceited. You are indeed wiser than I thought you were. But tell me, what would be the fastest way for a man to ride around the world?"

"If he rides at the same pace as the sun, it will take him no more than two times twelve hours," said Hans.

"Splendid, splendid!" cried the king. "But you will still ride on the back of the donkey through the whole land unless you tell me what I am thinking right now."

"You are thinking that I am the abbot," replied the shepherd. "But I am not. I am the abbot's shepherd, Hans, who asks you to forgive me my deceit. I knew of no other way to answer your questions."

"Where is the abbot?" the king asked.

"He is taking care of my sheep," Hans replied.

"Then let him stay with the sheep, and you take his place as the abbot," said the king. "I can see that you have more sense than he."

"Your Majesty," said Hans, "if you wish to please me, leave things as they are. I am happy with my sheep, and the abbot does a good job taking care of his abbey. I feel much closer to God when I am out in the fields than I ever would in the abbey. The abbot is my friend, and I know he will take care of me when I no longer can care for the sheep. And I ask for no more."

"I wish I were surrounded by friends like you," sighed

the king. "Go home to your abbot, and tell him he is a lucky man. But permit me to come to you whenever I need to get away from all my problems."

"I would be honored whenever you come," replied Hans, and he left and returned to his sheep. As the years passed, the king did come to see him, but during his visits he did not stay at the abbey. He stayed in the shepherd's simple hut, and when he left, he felt refreshed in body and spirit.

The Land Where No One Dies

Once there lived a young man who did not want to die. One day he said goodbye to his loved ones and went in search of a place where no one dies. The young man asked many people.

(Members of the audience can be asked to play the people.) Some people scolded him for looking for such a place. Others ridiculed him and called him foolish. The rest told him he was mad. Nobody knew of a place where no one died. The young man continued to search.

One day he met a man with a beard down to his chest who was pushing a wheelbarrow full of stones. The youth asked, "Old man, could you direct me to a place where no one dies?"

"Stay with me and help me," said the man. "Until I have finished tearing down this mountain, neither of us will die."

"How long will that take you?" asked the youth.

"About a hundred years," replied the old man.

"Will we die afterwards?" questioned the youth.

"We will be ready to die," said the old man.

"Not I," cried the youth. "I simply don't want to die. I will find a place where no one dies."

"Good luck to you," mumbled the old man, and he returned to his work while the youth walked on.

After many weeks the young man came to a forest that

144

seemed to have no end. At last he met another old man. His beard was hanging down to his waist, and he was pruning branches.

"Do you know of a place where no one dies?" asked the youth.

"Stay with me and help me," said the man. "Neither of us will die before we have finished pruning all the trees in this forest."

"How long will that take us?" asked the youth.

"About two hundred years," replied the old man.

"Will we die afterwards?" asked the youth.

"Of course we will die," said the old man. "No one lives forever."

"But I want to live forever!" cried the youth, and he continued his search.

After months and months of searching, he came to the seashore, where he met a man whose beard was hanging down to his knees. The man was watching a duck drinking water out of the ocean. "Could you tell me of a place where no one ever dies?" asked the youth.

"Stay with me," said the old man. "If you help me watch this duck, you won't die until she has drunk the sea dry."

"How long will that take?" asked the youth.

"About three hundred years," replied the old man.

"And we will die after that?" asked the youth.

"It will be time for us to die," said the old man.

"I don't want to die!" insisted the youth, and he continued his search.

At last he came to a palace. He entered it and met a very old man whose beard was hanging to his feet.

"Come in," said the old man. "It doesn't happen very often that someone takes the trouble to find me. This is the place where no one ever dies."

The youth was delighted. He moved into the palace and lived a long and pleasant life.

After many, many years had passed, the youth became restless and said to the old man, "I wonder how my family is doing. I would like to pay them a visit."

"Your parents died long ago," replied the old man.

"I still would like to see the old home. Maybe my brother's children's children are still living there," insisted the youth.

"Go then if you must," replied the old man. "Take my horse, which is as fast as the wind. But remember, never get out of the saddle, or you will die."

The youth mounted the horse and rode away. Soon he came to the place where the forest had been. There was not a single tree left. Nothing was there but prairie grass.

The same thing had happened with the sea. It had turned into a desert, and where the mountain had been there was flat land.

When the youth came home to his little village, everything looked different. He asked for his family, but no one remembered their name. The youth rode around for a while, but he found no pleasure in it. Sadly disappointed, the youth turned his horse to go back to his palace.

He had barely ridden a few miles when he met an old man who was trying to pull a cart of old shoes out of a rut.

"Give me a hand," cried the old man. "I can't get this cart out of the rut."

A strange feeling entered the youth's heart. The old man's request seemed like a command. Who was he to ask in such a way? the youth wondered.

"I must not get out of my saddle," replied the youth.

"You need not leave your saddle," said the old man. "Just put one foot down and help me pull."

There is no way to say no, thought the youth. He put one foot on the ground.

All of a sudden a bony hand grabbed his arm and the man said, "I am Death. What makes you think anyone can escape me? See all those shoes in the cart? These are all the pairs of shoes you caused me to wear out running after you. Don't you know one must make room for new people?"

The youth looked at Death, and Death did not seem terrible at all. "Take me," he said, "I am ready."

And Death took him.

The Hermit and the Robbers

There once lived a hermit who loved God. One day he decided to carve a chapel into a mountain so people could come and pray undisturbed. Using nothing but a hammer and a chisel, he began his work, and although the labor was hard and tiring, his heart was filled with joy. However, finding food every day took precious time away from his task, and one night he prayed for a solution to his problem.

The following day, while he was hammering and chiseling, a raven flew over his head and dropped a piece of bread. The hermit thanked the Lord and the raven, ate the bread, and rejoiced that he didn't have to go and look for food. From that day on, the raven brought food to him twice a day, and the hermit knew that God was pleased with his work.

The chapel took shape, and as the years passed, it became more and more beautiful. There were stone benches and an intricately carved stone altar. A star-shaped window over the entrance let the light in, and the walls were covered with carved scenes from the life of Jesus. Finally, there was only one more thing the hermit wanted to add—a stairway that led down to the valley.

One day, as he was busily carving out steps, he heard the sound of the "sinner's bell." He looked up and saw a hangman leading a man to the gallows.

"There goes a great sinner," said the hermit to himself. "It serves him right to be hanged. Why did he lead such an unholy life? If he had dedicated his life to God, as I have, he would not be facing such a terrible end."

The hermit thought no more of what he had said. But that evening the raven did not bring him any food. Nor did he bring anything to eat the next day or the day after. The hermit could have gone and searched for his own food, but he realized that there must be a reason for the raven's disappearance. He prayed, "Dear God, if I have offended you in any way, please let me know, so I can repent."

That night God spoke to him in his dream, saying, "You have done great injustice to the poor sinner who was being led to the gallows. Instead of feeling compassion, you judged him harshly, although you knew nothing about his life. If you want to atone, you must go and find a dead tree. Cut it down and keep the log. Carry that log out into the world and teach men and women to forgive one another. The day the dry log sprouts new leaves, you will know you are forgiven."

The hermit did as God had told him. It hurt him grievously to leave his beloved chapel, but he knew he had to go.

For years he walked from door to door and told the people that God is a God of love and compassion.

Some people listened and wanted to hear more about God. Others laughed at the hermit and chased him away from their doors.

It was a hard life, but as the hermit watched the men, women, and children and saw them struggling with life's problems, his love for them was reawakened. He began to understand God's patience and compassion.

One day, when no one had been willing to listen to his words, he wandered off into the forest. Night came, and he was just about to lie down and sleep beneath a tree when he saw a light. He walked toward it and came to a cave. An old woman sat in front of the cave.

"Please," said the hermit, "can you spare a bite of food and allow me to stay overnight?"

"I urge you to go away as fast as you can," cried the old woman. "I have three wicked and wild sons. If they find you, they will kill you."

But the hermit spoke kindly to the old woman, "Please let me stay. If it is God's will, something good will come of it."

When the old mother heard him speak so kindly, she let him in and gave him a bowl of soup. After the hermit had eaten, he lay down by the fire and put the log under his head.

"Why are you sleeping on a log?" asked the old woman.

"I am atoning for my sin," replied the hermit, and he told his story.

"Oh, woe to me! Oh, woe to my sons!" cried the old woman. "If God judges you so harshly for just a thought, how much more harshly will he judge them, for they are leading a wicked life. I am beginning to wish that neither I nor they had been born. But I am their mother, and I love them. In spite of their wickedness, I have never given up hope that one day they might change."

"Think for a moment," said the hermit. "If your love for your sons is already so great, how much greater must the love of God in heaven be? Let us pray for our souls and those of your sons."

Together they prayed, and afterward the hermit fell asleep.

In the early morning hours the sons returned to the hut. When they saw the stranger, the oldest son grabbed his mother by the shoulders, shook her, and whispered, "How dare you let a stranger in? Don't you know that we must kill him so he won't get away and tell the world about our hiding place?"

"Oh, leave him alone," said the old mother. "He is atoning for his sins."

"What did he do?" cried the sons. They woke up the hermit and asked him to tell them what he had done.

After the hermit had told his story, the sons began to cry. They confessed their sins. Together with the hermit they prayed for God's forgiveness.

Afterwards they went to sleep. When they awoke hours later, they found that the old man had died. But the log under his head had sprouted three green leaves, and the sons and their mother knew that God had forgiven him.

The Ox and His Master

Long ago in India, there lived a farmer who owned a very strong ox. During the day they toiled together in the fields, and when evening came the farmer fed the ox and said, "I thank you for working so hard for me, Brother Ox."

"I thank you for taking good care of me, Brother Man," replied the Ox, and they both enjoyed their hard-earned rest.

One day the farmer went to the market in a nearby village to sell some of his grain. Afterward he looked at some oxen that had been put up for sale. When he saw that none of them looked as strong as his, he said to the villagers there, "You should see my ox. He is so strong he could draw a line of one hundred carts."

The villagers laughed and said, "We bet you a hundred rupees he can't."

The farmer had not planned to bet on his ox. He knew if he lost a wager, he would have to borrow the money, and paying it back would be a great hardship. But he also knew how strong his ox was, so he replied, "It's a bet. I'll bring him tomorrow."

When he came home, he spoke to his ox. "Brother Ox, I went to the market today and took on a wager that you could draw a line of one hundred carts."

"It's going to be hard work," replied the ox. "But I will be glad to do it for you."

The next day the farmer took his ox to the village and found that all the people had come to see the ox who could draw a hundred carts. The carts were already in line, and as soon as the ox was yoked to the first, he planted his feet firmly on the ground and stood quietly to gather strength for the tremendous chore. The crowd, which was looking for excitement, misunderstood his stillness and began to yell:

> Hit him, hit him, make him sweat,
> Hit him so you won't lose your bet.

Incensed by their yelling, the farmer picked up a stick and began to beat his ox, shouting: "You lazy good-for-nothing rascal, what is the matter with you? Get going, show your strength."

The ox, who had never been beaten, was deeply humiliated. He put his head down, and neither the hard blows nor the angry words of his master could make him move.

At last the farmer had to admit his defeat. He promised to pay the hundred rupees the following day and took his ox home.

As the farmer led him to the shed, he said, "Brother Ox, why did you do that to me?"

"Do not call me brother," replied the ox sadly. "One does not beat one's brother, nor does one call him names or shame him in front of strangers."

When the farmer realized what he had done, he put his head on the ox's back and cried. At last he said, "Oh, Brother Ox, I don't know what came over me. Can you forgive me for beating you, and calling you names?"

"I can, if you will never beat me again," said the ox.

"I vow never to beat you again," cried the farmer.

"Listen to me then," said the ox. "Tomorrow I will go into the village and draw those hundred carts, so you can regain what you have lost."

The farmer was deeply moved by the generosity of his ox. The following morning he fed the ox a good meal and led him to the village. When they came to the market square the villagers came running and cried, "Why did you bring the ox? Are you going to bet again?"

"Indeed, I will," replied the farmer. "Today I will bet two hundred rupees that my ox can pull those hundred carts."

"We cannot tell you how to spend your money," said the villagers, and they gathered the carts and helped the farmer to yoke the ox to the first.

Once again the ox stood very still and concentrated on his task, and once again the people became restless and shouted

> Hit him, hit him, make him sweat,
> Hit him so you won't lose your bet.
>
> *(Audience joins in.)*

But this time the farmer stayed calm. He stroked the ox's sides, patted his head, and said gently, "Brother Ox, you and I know you can pull a hundred carts. Take your own good time."

The ox took his time, and when he was ready, he pulled with all his might. Soon the first cart began to move, then the second, and then the third, and in time the last cart stood where the first had been.

The villagers were amazed. They cheered like they had never cheered before. The women ran for flowers to make garlands for the ox, and the men reached into their pockets and collected the two hundred rupees.

The farmer said, "Let's use the money for a feast. I learned an important lesson today, and I want to celebrate."

The villagers were delighted, and when evening came, they gathered for a fine meal. During the meal the farmer told everyone why he was celebrating, and afterward all the little children got a ride on the back of Brother Ox.

Notes on the Stories

Part One

A Piece of the Wind

An African theology student wrote down this story for Ruthilde Kronberg and asked her to use it. Sometimes it takes children a while to grasp the idea of "ground and sifted water," or "a piece of the wind," but once they do, they enjoy the story as much as adults do.

The Woodpecker

This story is based on a Rumanian folktale.

Your Room, My Room

Here is an original story by Frederick and Patricia McKissack that illustrates how to allow another person self-expression while not compromising your own tastes and needs.

The Wise Shepherd Boy

This German story is retold from Grimm's fairy tales. The children can be encouraged to recall the three questions the shepherd boy must answer.

Tante Tina

This German folktale can be heard on radio on the *Springboard to Learning* program "Heroes, Heroes, Everywhere" through the Intercollegian Broadcast System. A similar Asian story is "Burning of the Rice Fields."

The King's Cathedral

This German folktale is based on the Bible story of the widow's offering in Mark 12:41–44. The Christmas story "Why the Chimes Rang," by R. M. Alden has a similar theme.

Now That I Have a Green Thumb

This original story by Frederick and Patricia McKissack deals with the age-old problem of thumb sucking in a humorous way. It may help parents of small children learn to overcome a problem with love and kindness rather than with punishment.

Bundles of Worries, Bundles of Blessings

Ruthilde Kronberg heard this story as a child in Europe. You may wish to ask members of the audience to talk about their own worries and blessings or make an (anonymous) list of them.

The Mirror

This Japanese story is a good one to retell with members of the audience miming the parts.

The Very Good Samaritan

A favorite of boys and girls at a juvenile detention center, this story comes from Spain. You might compare it with the biblical story of Luke 10:30–37.

The Street Sweeper

The Middle East is the birthplace of this story, which comes down to us through oral tradition. As a follow-up activity, you could suggest that children write letters to the merchant, the street sweeper, the little girl, and her mother.

A King Seeks God

This Russian tale is based on a story by Leo Tolstoy. The audience can keep track of the questions and answers in the story.

Part Two

The Legend of Tutokanula

Native Americans first told this tale of the inchworm, Tutokanula (tu-tok-a-NOO-la). You can make up your own melody to the song. Tell, sing, and dance the story with children.

The Rabbit and the Elephant

This tale comes from Ghana in West Africa. You may make up your own melody or chant for the song and have the audience join you. After hearing the story, children can act it out.

The Day Justice Died

A man is cheated out of his land but finds justice in the end in this German folktale. Before you tell the story, teach the audience the refrain, "Sun, dim your light. Justice has died."

The Toy Maker

This story by Ruthilde Kronberg gives children insight into the life of the hearing impaired. Have children sit on chairs in a circle. Include one or two extra chairs in the circle. Assign the children roles. Let the first child be a dancing doll; the second, a growling bear; the third, a rabbit who can hop; the fourth, another dancing doll; and so on. Explain that whenever you sign their new name, each of them must quietly find another chair. To sign *dancing* form a V with index and middle finger, indicating legs, and move "legs" back and forth over the open palm of the opposite hand. For *doll* you can place your right hand in the crook of your left arm, as if rocking a baby.

To sign *growling* use facial expressions. For *bear* place tips of fingernails into outer chest. Keep nails there, but wiggle arms back and forth.

To sign *rabbits* place both hands at the sides of the head with palms facing back. Move fingers up and down to represent the ears of a rabbit. To sign *hop* use the same gesture as for *dancing*, only make the "legs" hop. The children may mime their characters by dancing (*dolls*), hopping (*rabbits*), or shuffling (*bears*). If they bump into one another, they must leave the circle for two minutes.

Turtle and Her Pesky Friends

In this original story by Ruthilde Kronberg a kind turtle

teaches her pesky friends a lesson. To enhance this story use a toy turtle, spider, snake, and mouse, available from variety stores. Teach the *coochatta* refrain before you tell the story.

The Queen Bee

This German folktale is retold from Grimm's fairy tales. After you've told the story the first time, reenact the whole story or selected scenes. Choose children to play the major parts.

What Is the Value of a Prayer?

In this German folktale a steward learns a hard lesson. After telling the story, choose a nobleman, a steward, an old man, and a hermit. Choose scenes from the story and act them out.

Part Three

The Starling's Song

This is an original Christmas story by Ruthilde Kronberg. The story can be told, but it is more fun to play it with children.

Characters should sit on chairs according to the diagram below. On their journey to Bethlehem the children walk within the circle each time they travel and sit down during dialogues. Only Josiah and Judah go straight to a nativity picture or transparency after they have said their parts.

STORYTELLER   NATIVITY PICTURE

AMOS   JUDAH

JUDAH   JOSIAH

JOSIAH   LION

REUBEN   DOG

ABIGAIL   CAT

STARLING   STARLING

STARLING   STARLING

STARLING

God Is Greater Than the King

This African story can be staged the same way as "The Starling's Song." Arrange players in a circle as shown in the diagram below.

STORYTELLER

OSEI	PEOPLE
OPALANGA	PEOPLE
OSEI'S SON	PEOPLE
SPY	PEOPLE

KING

Gold-Lillie and Spider-Millie

Ruthilde Kronberg, who wrote this story, says, "When I play or retell this story with children, I put the main players in a row of chairs facing the audience:"

STORYTELLER

→   →   →   →   →   →

FATHER	MILLIE	LILLIE	BERRY BUSH	WALNUT TREE	OLD WOMAN	CAT	DOG

←   ←   ←   ←   ←   ←
DOLL   DOLL
    DOLL   DOLL
      DOLL   DOLL
          DOLL   DOLL
              DOLL   DOLL

AUDIENCE

All the movement is done around the chairs. The remaining children are the dolls and stay in their seats.

Peck a Hole to Chinaland

This story by Ruthilde Kronberg follows the same directions as those for "Gold-Lillie and Spider-Millie." Players may be seated in a row in this order:

→   →   →   →   →   →

WOMAN	VALERIE	DANIEL	FARMER & MRS. PETERSON	MAYOR & MRS. SIMEON	GOVERNOR & MRS. ANDREW	PRESIDENT ACHIM

←   ←   ←   ←   ←   ←

STORYTELLER

AUDIENCE

Arrows indicate movement around chairs. The rest of the audience play the Chinese people and chant along.

Bad Uncle Rat

This story by Ruthilde Kronberg can be used to teach awareness of drug abuse. It can be staged in the same way as the two previous stories. Seat players in this order:

→   →   →   →   →   →

RAT MOTHER MOUSE SISTER BROTHER CAT DOG FOX BEAR

←   ←   ←   ←   ←   ←

STORYTELLER

AUDIENCE

You may play the story more than once with children taking turns at playing the main characters.

Part Four

The Christmas Quilt

Ruthilde Kronberg wrote this story to deal more positively with the figure of the stepmother, an important concept in this day of blended families.

Budulinek

The Czech story of Budulinek (Bu-DOO-lin-ek) can open the way for a discussion of safety rules for children.

The Shipwrecked Merchant

This story, retold from a Hasidic tale, has a wonderful surprise ending.

Small Fry

Patricia McKissack wrote this story based on Plato's myth of the cave. She has used it with very young children and with adults. It is an excellent discussion starter regarding beliefs, prejudices, and personal limitations.

Kind Ivan

Here is a gentle Easter story by Ruthilde Kronberg. The audience may join in on the repeated line: "If that's what you want to do, I will not stop you."

The King and the Abbot

This story, based on an old German ballad, again raises three questions. It can be compared with other "riddling" stories.

The Land Where No One Dies

Based on an Italian folktale, this story can lead children into a wholesome discussion about death as a natural part of life. It is also a good story to retell and act out.

The Hermit and the Robbers

Another story based on the fairy tales of the brothers Grimm, this tale can be used to discuss the death penalty with an audience of older children and adults.

The Ox and His Master

This story from India can be used to initiate conversation about abuse of animals or human beings.

Both authors are available to lead workshops on storytelling.

Ruthilde Kronberg, 605 Bacon Avenue, Webster Groves, MO 63119.

Patricia C. McKissack, 225 S. Meramec Avenue, Suite 206, Clayton, MO 63105.